HIGH DRAMA

COLORADO'S HISTORIC THEATRES

By Daniel & Beth R. Barrett

*To Jan,
the Queen of Drama
Beth Barrett*

WESTERN REFLECTIONS PUBLISHING COMPANY®

Montrose, CO

ISBN-13: 978-1-932738-18-6
ISBN-10: 1-932738-18-5

Library of Congress Control Number: 2005932059

Cover and text design: Laurie Goralka Design

First Edition
Printed in the United States of America

Western Reflections Publishing Company®
219 Main Street
Montrose, CO 81401
www.westernreflectionspub.com

DEDICATION

My husband, Dan, died a few weeks before this manuscript was accepted for publication. His lifelong passion for nineteenth-century theatre history resulted in a previous book, many articles, and longstanding collegial relationships with scholars in the field. Dan was especially fond of this project, and I have happy memories of the many days we spent together, piecing Colorado's theatre history into this book. Dan worked on the manuscript throughout the six-month illness that preceded his death. Just ten days before he died, in fact, he spent hours fact-checking this text at the Western History Department of the Denver Public Library.

Like his commitment to *High Drama*, Dan's dedication to his family and friends was formidable. His courage in confronting late-stage cancer gave all of us who knew him a new definition of grace in facing the incomprehensibility of an untimely death. While I grieve for Dan, I know he would be delighted that this decade-long effort is seeing its way into print.

This book is dedicated to Dan, whose incandescent spirit lit my way for almost thirty years.

Beth Barrett

TABLE OF CONTENTS

Dedication 3
Preface 7
Acknowledgments 9

CHAPTER 1
Introduction: The Colorado Theatre Boom 11

CHAPTER 2
Central City 29

CHAPTER 3
Denver 51
   Tabor Grand Opera House
   Broadway Theatre
   Elitch's Gardens Theatre

CHAPTER 4
Leadville and Aspen 83
   Tabor Opera House
   Wheeler Opera House

CHAPTER 5
Colorado Springs and Pueblo 111
   Colorado Springs Opera House
   Burns Theatre
   Pueblo Grand Opera House

CHAPTER 6
Representative Theatres of Colorado 143

CHAPTER 7
The Melodrama Tradition in Colorado:
A Link to the Past 169

Appendix A: Colorado's Historic Theatres: A Chronology 179
For Further Reading 183
Notes 189
Index 197

PREFACE

Colorado's rich theatre history made itself apparent to us practically from the first day we set foot in the state. In the lobby of the hotel where we stayed while looking for a house, we were astonished to find a brochure for an obscure nineteenth-century melodrama, alive and well and being produced in Cripple Creek. Before long, we found other evidence of early theatre. The beautifully restored opera houses at Central City and Aspen, with their vibrant, modern-day festivals, convinced us that Colorado possessed an uncommon theatrical legacy. As we began to explore less well-known theatres, we discovered ghosts: vanished theatres with colorful histories that remained largely untold and unillustrated.

Although others have explored the state's theatrical past, no one devoted as much effort to it as did Benjamin Poff Draper (1907-1980). A professor of broadcast communications at San Francisco State University and the recipient of several Emmy Awards as a television producer, Ben Draper began his study of Colorado theatres in 1936. He spent summers in Georgetown for most of his life; the house he lived in still bears a testimonial plaque. Through the years, he painstakingly collected information on every theatre in the state, from early tent theatres to drive-ins, arranging them in an alphabetical list by city. His research culminated in a magisterial, five-volume dissertation, "Colorado Theatres, 1859-1969," for which he received a Ph.D. (his second) from the University of Denver. In 1975, five years prior to his death on his seventy-third birthday, he generously donated his collection of theatre materials to the Western History Collection of the Denver Public Library. Draper's dissertation on Colorado theatre is still not widely known and is not even mentioned in several standard theatre bibliographies. Yet it served as a much appreciated starting point throughout our research, and we owe him our gratitude and admiration.

Two final notes. Throughout the book we have chosen to use the spelling "theatre" rather than "theater." Although present-day Americans tend to use the latter, theatre historians generally prefer "theatre," as did our nineteenth-century ancestors in America.

Last, a note on contemporaneous newspaper reviews. Many are sprinkled with ungrammatical usage and creative spellings, but we have often opted to leave them as written, uninterrupted with "[*sic*]"s. We felt that the flavor of the times is better caught without reminding readers of the possible shortcomings of the age's writers and typesetters.

ACKNOWLEDGMENTS

Researchers in Colorado theatre history have access to not one but two outstanding collections, conveniently located across the street from one another: the Western History Collection at Denver Public Library (with its splendid Gates Reading Room) and the Stephen H. Hart Library at the Colorado Historical Society. We would especially like to thank Philip J. Panum, Bruce Hanson, Barbara Walton, Lisa Backman, and other staff members of the Denver Public Library, as well as Ruba Sadi and Jennifer Bosley of the Colorado Historical Society, for their helpfulness, courtesy, and efficiency in tracking down obsure documents and responding to our many requests. Information provided from the Colorado Historical Society's State Historical Fund by James Stratis regarding current renovation projects was also most helpful.

We are also grateful to the following individuals and institutions that have aided our research and, in many cases, gone to great lengths to provide us with information and photographs: in Boulder, Marty Covey and David M. Hays, Archives, University of Colorado Library; in Central City, JoAnn Sims and Becky Lathrop; in Colorado Springs, Sharron G. Uhler and Leah Davis, Colorado Springs Pioneers Museum; Tim Blevins and Nancy Thaler, Pikes Peak Library District; in Cripple Creek, Wayne Mackin; in Grand Junction, Judy Prosser-Armstrong, Museum of Western Colorado; in Ouray, Doris H. Gregory; Alice and Larry Leeper; in Pueblo, Noreen I. Riffe, Special Collections, Pueblo Library District; Madge Gaylord; Lloyd C. Engelbrecht; in Salida, Donna Nevens; Judy Micklich, Salida Museum; and in Trinidad, Glenn R. Aultman. At the Huntington Library, Cathy Cherbosque and Erin Chase; at the University of Washington, Chris Kinsey; and at the University of Texas in Austin, Rick Watson.

Finally, we would like to thank our children, Mark and Judith, who have shared our love of Colorado theatre. In this endeavor, as in all others, they are our inspiration.

CHAPTER ONE

INTRODUCTION:
The Colorado Theatre Boom

Colorado's theatrical legacy is as rich as the state's fabled mining history, and not surprisingly, the two are related. Westward expansion in the Kansas Territory became frantic once gold was discovered at Cherry Creek in 1858 and a year later at Chicago Creek and Gregory Gulch, high in the Rocky Mountains. Tens of thousands of people, armed with picks, shovels, and pans, headed for what was called the Pikes Peak region. The earliest arrivals lived in tents and hastily constructed buildings that offered little protection from the long, harsh winters. As surface deposits played out, gold seekers moved on, tantalized by announcements of finds in Montana, Nevada, and elsewhere. Population in the Colorado Territory, formed in 1861, slowly declined, until by 1870 it stood at about 40,000.[1] Statehood arrived in 1876 amid more rumors of rich strikes, this time of silver. The silver boom was slower to take off, since the finding and transporting of silver-bearing ore was not a one-man, get-rich-quick enterprise. Still, as it became clear there were fortunes waiting in the mountains, the stampede began again. Dusty, one-time boomtowns exploded to renewed life; new tent cities cropped up wherever the digging looked promising.

As the settlements grew more permanent, they began to take on the accouterments of their Eastern neighbors. Each town sought to provide a modicum of culture and sophistication for its residents by establishing amateur drama and singing groups, holding lecture series, and hosting touring entertainers. Rudimentary theatres sprang up from the plains to the mountains.

The word "theatre," however, often had an unwholesome ring to the ears of our pioneer ancestors, and many nineteenth-century Americans regarded the term with suspicion. Their circumspection is hardly surprising, considering that everything from a dance hall to a saloon was referred to as a theatre. Commonly found on the upper floors of drinking and gambling halls, theatres were routinely inveighed against by religious leaders as havens of vice. Few women who valued their reputations attended them. A question of semantics arose: how to distinguish between bawdy, low-class entertainment houses and the socially acceptable, legitimate theatre? Many towns settled the issue by designating their foremost playhouse as the "opera house," fully realizing that opera might be an infrequent visitor. Since musical programs and concerts did not suffer the same negative connotations as theatre did, a performance hall called an "opera house" avoided the questionable associations of one designated a "theatre." The obvious high culture bestowed by the term made it clear that civilization had arrived, and that the best entertainment a town could offer would be found on its stage.

From today's perspective, it seems puzzling that small and isolated towns should have had such grandiose aspirations. However, in 1870, Central City's population was second only to Denver's in the Colorado Territory.[2] Leadville ranked second by 1880.[3] By 1890, Pueblo, with its railroad connections and industrial clout, seemed poised to become a regional transportation and smelting center, ready to challenge Denver for the distinction of Colorado's principal city. Every mining camp saw itself as tomorrow's metropolis, possibly at the forefront of the state's future. And every potential city needed a lavish theatre as a symbol of wealth and refinement, a testament to its lasting commitment to the cultural life of its citizens. Early Coloradans tended to be practical sorts, though, and many towns managed to combine opulence with versatility. Theatres often served as community centers and needed the flexibility of movable seating and level auditorium floors. A popular combination was the rink theatre, such as those in Grand Junction and Aspen, which operated as roller rinks between theatrical engagements.

Gold and silver brought the settlers, but the railroads brought civilization. Developed from the economic need to move ore to cities and hard-rock mining equipment to the mountains, the railroads followed the rich strikes. Railroads also brought all manner of commodities, from the latest fashions to theatrical productions with casts no longer confined to a single theatre. Towns that managed to get a railroad connection knew they had advanced from hustling camps to real towns and cities.

The Rockies were a formidable obstacle to the construction of a transcontinental railroad. The first to link the coasts, a joint venture of the Union Pacific and Central Pacific Railroads, threaded its way through them and clipped only the northeast corner of what is now

Colorado before completion in 1869. But the gold strikes of the late 1850s made railroad access an urgent need, especially since Colorado lacked a navigable river system. Denver soon became the railroading hub of Colorado, connecting cargo and passengers from one coast to another. In the 1870s, William Jackson Palmer took dead aim at the rich mining resources of Leadville and lucrative points west with his narrow-gauge Denver & Rio Grande Railroad. Palmer and the D&RG pre-vailed in gaining access from Canon City to Leadville in a conflict with the Atchison, Topeka & Santa Fe Railroad over the narrow chasm of the Royal Gorge, an altercation that brought armed guards and sabotage to the canyon and wound up being resolved by the U.S. Supreme Court in favor of the Denver & Rio Grande in 1879.

Narrow-gauge construction fit Palmer's needs, as well as those of the competing Colorado Central and Denver, South Park & Pacific: track was cheaper to build, since it was only three feet between rails instead of the standard-gauge four feet, eight and one-half inches, and the narrower width enabled the correspondingly smaller trains to navigate tight mountain turns. In addition, the need for expensive tunnels or extensions on narrow mountain ledges was reduced.[4] The tortuous but economical routes of the narrow-gauge lines took traveling theatre troupes through many of the booming mountain towns, where they stopped to keep money coming in on their way to the West Coast.

Mountain entertainment was an arduous profession before the advent of railroads. Like the well-known mountain trouper Jack Langrishe and his company, most actors traveled from camp to camp on uncertain roads by wagon or stagecoach. Transportation of stage prop-erties was limited, leaving companies to utilize whatever was at hand when they arrived at their destinations, not uncommonly a tent or other makeshift arrangement to house them for their short stay. Langrishe, an Irishman born in 1829, arrived in Denver in September 1860 with his company for what was billed as a six-day engagement. He remained for twenty-five years, although he and his company sometimes disappeared from the state for years at a time to tour elsewhere. Immensely popular from the start, Langrishe was largely responsible for shaping Colorado's theatrical sensibilities. He quickly moved from performing in a room above a saloon, to an authentic, if basic, theatre and proceeded to offer an extensive range of plays, from Shakespearean tragedy to melodrama and comedy. The company typically performed seven times each week in constantly changing repertory. In contrast, its accompanying three-piece "orchestra" had a severely limited range, using the same music over and over, regardless of the play. Langrishe was producer, actor, manager,

Jack Langrishe (1829–1895),
"The Father of Colorado Theatre,"
in costume as O'Callaghan in
His Last Legs

director, and owner. Loved especially for his comic portrayals, he was game for almost any part. When his wife, an actress in the company, was once unable to go on, Langrishe took her part, much to the delight of the audience. A pattern developed, with the troupe spending November through April in Denver and then going to the mountains to tour mining camps for the spring and summer on "the Gold Circuit." They spent relatively long periods in Central City but also toured as far afield as New England, California, and Mexico. Langrishe apparently was uncomfortable with the encroachment of city life, and in 1885 he left Colorado for good, heading for the frontier in Idaho. He died there in 1895, having founded countless theatres throughout the West, and earned the appellation "The Father of Colorado Theatre."[5]

Aided by the growth of the railroads, the late nineteenth century was the golden age of touring theatre companies. In the Rocky Mountains, no one played a more important role than Peter McCourt, Jr.. McCourt had been hired by Horace Tabor to be his personal secretary after Tabor's marriage in 1883 to Peter's sister, Elizabeth "Baby Doe" McCourt. Tabor turned over the management of the Tabor Grand Opera House in Denver to McCourt in 1884 after having a falling out with his previous manager, William H. Bush. McCourt realized he was limited in the East Coast attractions he could entice to journey to the Tabor Grand alone, so he began signing up theatres throughout the Front Range into an early booking circuit. As railroads connected more and more towns, McCourt continued adding theatres to his circuit until they stretched to Salt Lake City and Laramie, Wyoming. Resort towns such as Colorado Springs and Glenwood Springs shared attractions with smelter centers (Pueblo, for example) and such farming communities as Grand Junction to form, with the burgeoning mountain mining towns,

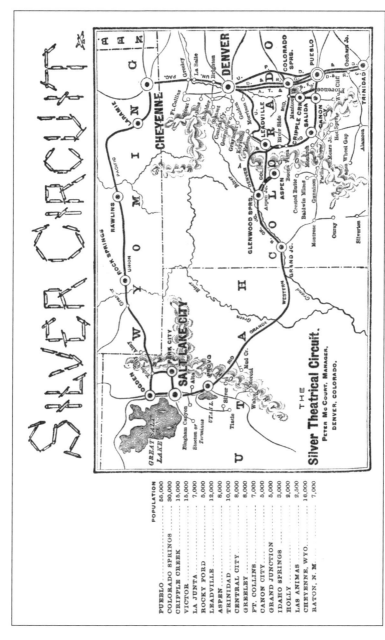

The theatres of the Silver Theatrical Circuit, c. 1893. The number of theatres fluctuated from year to year.

PHOTO COURTESY COLORADO HISTORICAL SOCIETY, F37909

what McCourt called the Silver Theatrical Circuit. Several years in the planning, the Silver Circuit was officially launched in the spring of 1889. By 1891, seventeen theatres in Colorado, Wyoming, and Utah had signed with McCourt, who acted as a booking agent for all.[6]

Companies rarely visited all the towns on the Circuit; instead, they usually followed one of three major routes through the Rockies, using a combination of the narrow-gauge railroads as well as the standard-gauge Union Pacific, Atchison, Topeka & Santa Fe, and Colorado Midland Railroads. This arrangement worked well for touring groups, for whom coast-to-coast engagements had previously been financially unfeasible. The Silver Circuit offered the possibility of playing Denver for a week, then embarking on a series of largely one-night stands through smaller towns on the way to Salt Lake City or San Francisco. The costs of making the long journey to the West Coast were considerably defrayed, and some tours even made money on the way to their destinations. Eventually, McCourt had groups traveling in both directions over the mountains, and it became possible for a troupe to take one itinerary on the way out and another on the return, so that doubling back was minimized and new theatres could be played on each leg of the trip.[7]

Until the Silver Crash of 1893, McCourt held a virtual monopoly on which groups were booked and where they played throughout the Rockies. With fellow managers and business associates Alf Hayman and Charles Frohman, he controlled theatre in the West. Not that the Circuit always functioned smoothly: McCourt had to deal with troupes that were stranded by heavy mountain snows, scenery that was lost or sent to the wrong city, trains that derailed or ran behind schedule, and companies that suddenly disbanded in the middle of a tour. Sometimes stars refused to play small towns and substituted understudies at the last minute. Even ladies' hats became a contentious issue, when in the mid-1890s they became so large that those sitting behind them could not see. Decorously worded notices appeared in programs, suggesting that a lady's crowning glory was her hair—not her hat. More seriously, McCourt was plagued for many years by labor problems, with frequent strikes by stagehands and musicians. Most dangerous of all was the threat of fire, which demolished a number of theatres during the heyday of the Silver Circuit and left McCourt scrambling for replacement theatres in which to schedule his productions.[8]

McCourt was chiefly responsible for what Colorado theatregoers saw for forty years, until his death in 1929. His influence lessened over the years, as the New York Theatrical Syndicate and the Schubert brothers gained control over nationwide theatre bookings. Principally remembered today as the wealthy but uncaring brother who let Baby Doe live out her long life alone and penniless (a fate his actions and letters contradict), McCourt was one of a handful of Coloradans who were instrumental in shaping the state's theatrical legacy.

Peter McCourt (1859-1929), manager of the Silver Theatrical Circuit (date unknown). He bore a strong resemblance to his famous sister, Baby Doe, second wife of Horace Tabor.
PHOTO COURTESY COLORADO HISTORICAL SOCIETY, F749

William H. Bush (1829-1898), first manager of the Tabor Opera House in Leadville and the Tabor Grand Opera House in Denver (date unknown).
PHOTO COURTESY COLORADO HISTORICAL SOCIETY, F10017

Ironically, one of those with whom McCourt's name is permanently linked is his onetime rival, William H. Bush. Bush was one of Colorado's most distinguished hotel proprietors, beginning in the 1870s, when he owned Central City's fabled Teller House. After becoming acquainted with Horace Tabor in 1878, Bush moved to Leadville the following year and became Tabor's close associate. In addition to owning the plush Clarendon Hotel there, he also assumed management of Tabor's opera house. He followed Tabor to Denver as business and politics drew Horace away from Leadville, and became the first manager of the resplendent Tabor Grand Opera House when it opened in 1881. Bush's association with Tabor lasted until the latter's bitter divorce from his first wife, Augusta, in 1883. Bush acted as Tabor's unwilling mediator with her, receiving the brunt of her considerable temper. Although he had little sympathy for Augusta, Bush advised Tabor against the divorce, feeling it would jeopardize Tabor's political career. His opposition probably cost him his place as Tabor's business partner. Tabor sued Bush over opera house profits and replaced him with his new brother-in-law, Peter McCourt. Out of Tabor's employ, Bush moved on to manage the Windsor Hotel, one of Denver's finest. In 1892, he became the first manager of the luxurious Brown Palace Hotel in Denver, which he had helped to build.[9]

While he continued to manage hotels, Bush's interest in theatre management had not abated. When offered the opportunity to become part owner of a proposed theatre fabulous enough to compete with the Tabor Grand, Bush immediately signed on, even suggesting the site, across Seventeeth Street from the plot upon which the Brown Palace would be built. Bush acted as manager of the resulting Broadway Theatre for many years, eventually hiring Peter McCourt when Tabor lost the mortgage on the Tabor Grand in 1896 and McCourt was let go. McCourt and Bush apparently harbored no animosity toward one another and worked together closely until Bush's unexpected death in 1898. Bush's plans to put together another theatre circuit that would have stretched to the Southwest, challenging the growing influence of the Syndicate, died with him.[10]

Managers McCourt and Bush booked entertainment of every kind into their Denver theatres and onto the Silver Circuit. Sometimes entire Broadway productions, with cast, crew, and properties intact, decamped from New York for a cross-country tour. The popular plays of Charles Hoyt, such as *A Texas Steer* and *A Stranger in New York*, made their way to Colorado stages a year after they played on Broadway during the 1880s and 1890s. Some of the most famous companies, notably those run by impresarios Charles and Daniel Frohman, Augustin Daly, and Lester Wallack, toured extensively out of their New York theatres and engaged nationally known actors and actresses, such as Ada Rehan and Rose Coghlan. The highly regarded touring ensemble known as The Bostonians performed light opera productions to packed houses; their gross receipts at the Tabor Grand set records. In addition to dramatic and operatic productions, there were touring minstrel shows, vaudeville and burlesque troupes, circuses, and boxing and magic exhibitions.[11]

The Colorado Midland Railroad traverses Hells Gate carrying popular singer Anna Held (center) and her entourage, 1904.
PHOTO COURTESY COLORADO HISTORICAL SOCIETY, CHS B1393

As railroads proliferated across the country (40,000 miles of track were added from 1870 to 1880), the lure of ready audiences and lucrative tours induced many famous stars to put up with the long train trips and uncertain stage facilities promised by a road trip. Edwin Booth, the famous tragedian, kept eighty-five per cent of the house receipts when he toured, making it a far more profitable endeavor for him than for the manager who struggled to cover costs with the remaining fifteen per cent.[12] Actors past their prime, finding it difficult to land roles in New York, often closed out their careers on the road, capitalizing on their still-recognized names. Stars and their accompanying troupes often competed with, or displaced, established touring companies.[13] The actors of the venerable Milton Nobles Company crisscrossed the West for many years, performing a musty, old-fashioned repertoire until increased competition forced them out of the legitimate theatre and onto the vaudeville circuit. By that time, theatregoers in Colorado had seen some of the greatest actors of the age: Lawrence Barrett, Otis Skinner, Helena Modjeska, and Sarah Bernhardt all appeared before rapt audiences. Touring productions flourished until the iron-handed New York Theatrical Syndicate effectively strangled the life out of the system. Film, cheap and easy to transport, delivered the coup de grâce by turning live road shows into expensive relics of a past age.

Shakespeare was performed more often than any other playwright, although the Bard's plays sometimes drew smaller crowds than those for other, less rarefied productions. Lawrence Barrett and Edwin Booth often appeared in Shakespearean tragedies as well as in romantic dramas of the age, such as *Richelieu* and *The Lady of Lyons*. Acclaimed actor Robert Mantell, prohibited from crossing the New York state line because of an alimony judgment, toured successfully in a variety of Shakespearean roles for many years.[14] One accepted practice, which by today's standards seems bizarre, was that of famous European actors performing Shakespeare in their native tongues, while the rest of the company spoke their lines in English, as when Tommaso Salvini appeared on the stage of the Tabor Grand in *Othello* in March 1886.[15]

Melodrama was a favorite with audiences. *East Lynne, Hazel Kirke,* and *Fanchon the Cricket* were three of the most frequently performed works in this genre, which featured one-dimensional cruel villains and beleaguered heroines. Most dealt with social issues of the day, although society's ills were often summed up in the evil character of the villain, rather than portrayed as a wider phenomenon. Also popular were sensation dramas, many of which included references to the latest gizmos of the day, as well as spectacular scenes that showed the ingenuity of lighting hands, carpenters, and stage crews. This appetite for effect is still with us today in the crashing chandelier of *The Phantom of the Opera* and the worthy felines of *Cats* ascending to the Heavyside Layer.

A good example of a sensation drama is *The Octoroon*, a work by the age's most popular playwright, Dion Boucicault. Boucicault, born in Dublin in 1822, wrote plays that found wide audiences in London and

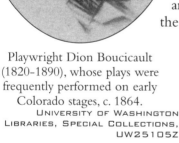

Playwright Dion Boucicault (1820-1890), whose plays were frequently performed on early Colorado stages, c. 1864.

New York. He spent considerable time in America and wound up moving here in the 1870s. In *The Octoroon*, a play set about 1860 in Louisiana, Boucicault takes on the issue of slavery. He includes two sensational scenes, one of a slave auction and the other of the sinking of a river steamboat. The plot also includes the vindication of an accused murderer when the lens of a camera, a new invention at the time, conveniently, and with no human intervention, captures an image of the actual culprit committing the crime.

The Octoroon drew on the same themes as the most performed play of all, *Uncle Tom's Cabin*. Hundreds of companies toured in "Tom shows" late in the century, sometimes trying to outdo each other in size and spectacle. Sutton's Monster Double Company, for example, performed the play in Colorado in 1892 and boasted "thirty-two artists, . . . two educated donkeys, four Cuban bloodhounds, and four Shetland ponies."[16]

Musical entertainment was also popular across the state. A perennial favorite was John Philip Sousa and his band, which toured Colorado almost yearly near the turn of the century. Light opera, such as the sprightly French opera-bouffe championed by Maurice Grau, drew appreciative, if select, audiences. Foreign language light opera was eclipsed, however, when the fabulously popular English operettas of Gilbert and Sullivan burst upon the scene in the late 1870s and 1880s. Dozens of companies toured pirated versions of *H.M.S. Pinafore*, in the absence of adequate copyright laws. Other now-forgotten operettas were written or translated to capitalize on the rage for Gilbert and Sullivan, echoes of which can still be heard today in such songs as "O Promise Me" and "Reuben, Reuben, I've Been Thinking."[17]

John Philip Sousa (1854-1932) frequently appeared with his band in Colorado's theatres.
COURTESY OF THE HUNTINGTON LIBRARY, SAN MARINO, CALIFORNIA

Grand opera also filled the stages of the opera houses of Colorado. Adelina Patti and Nellie Melba created sensations when they appeared, filling houses despite unheard-of ticket prices of up to $5.00. The Metropolitan Opera Company came in 1900, setting box office records for its production of *Lohengrin*. Most of the nation's opera companies in the late nineteenth century were touring troupes, often specializing in a particular repertory. The Lambardi Opera Company, for example, presented popular Italian mainstays, while Walter Damrosch's troupe performed German stalwarts. Others championed opera sung in English translation. Many of the most famous companies were headed by women. Emma Abbott, called "the populist prima donna," and Emma Juch were both singer-impressarias who toured extensively with their companies. Miss Abbott, whose abilities and penchant for interpolating popular songs into unsuspecting operas were dimly viewed by critics, nevertheless was extraordinarily popular with American audiences. Her company was chosen to open the Tabor Grand Opera House in Denver, while Miss Juch's company inaugurated the competing Broadway Theatre when it opened nine years later.[18]

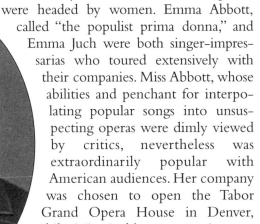

Tommaso Salvini (1829-1916) toured the West performing Shakespeare in his native Italian (date unknown).
COURTESY OF THE HUNTINGTON LIBRARY, SAN MARINO, CALIFORNIA

Less weighty than opera and its cousins were the popular, related forms of minstrelsy, vaudeville, and burlesque. All three featured loosely structured acts or sets with a series of performers doing musical numbers and skits. Minstrelsy, popular before the Civil War, continued its curious life in road shows. Some minstrel shows had African-American performers, but most presented whites imitating blacks in exaggerated, burnt-cork makeup and heavy dialect that reinforced the age's negative stereotypes. Minstrel shows grew from small companies portraying reassuring (to their white audiences, anyway) scenes of happy plantation life, to extravaganzas with large casts, glittering costumes and sets, and lavish production numbers.[19] Haverly's Minstrels, the most famous of the latter variety, appeared often on Colorado stages through the turn of the century.

Succeeding minstrelsy in popularity was vaudeville, an inexpensive, family-oriented collection of song and dance acts. Burlesque, an older dramatic form, eventually shared many characteristics with vaudeville, although its character was considerably less chaste: most burlesque

A composite photo of the cast of Haverly's Original Mastodon Minstrels.

troupes owed their popularity to the ample exposure of women's legs and were attended by almost exclusively male audiences.

Not all theatre in the Centennial State was aimed at its English-speaking residents. Almost seventeen per cent of those living in Colorado in 1870 were immigrants; mining towns and Denver had especially large foreign-born populations. Although little evidence remains of their entertainment, one obvious example survives in Denver—the West Denver Turn Halle, now a part of the Tivoli complex that houses the Auraria Campus's Student Union at Tenth and Larimer Streets. Built in 1882 as part of the Colorado Brewery complex, the Turn Halle was designed as part gymnasium, part theatre. There were a number of Turnvereins, or gymnastics clubs, in nineteenth-century Colorado towns that had German populations large enough to support them. Leadville, Central City, and Pueblo all had Turnvereins, along with several that flourished in Denver. The West Denver Turn Halle was designed by prominent local architect Harold W. Baerresen and could seat about one thousand on a flat auditorium floor and horseshoe balcony. Touring groups appeared sporadically, so most productions were home talent musical offerings performed in German. Although the brewery complex that houses the hall underwent a number of changes of ownership, "Turners," as members were called, used the hall for plays, concerts, lectures, and balls until the 1940s. Today the theatre is still in use by students, faculty, and community groups. While it is not completely restored, it looks much as it did in the 1880s, having survived threats to tear it down in the 1970s and a fire in the 1980s. With its small stage, "golden horseshoe," and multipurpose auditorium, it is a good example of what many early theatres looked like throughout Colorado.[20]

Colorado's explosive growth in the latter half of the nineteenth century relied heavily on mining. But the silver boom became a victim of its own success as supply outstripped demand and prices fell. Unwilling to submit to market economics, free silver backers persuaded Congress to pass the Sherman Silver Purchase Act in July 1890, which provided massive subsidies to the silver industry. Under the act's provisions, the government was required to buy vast quantities of new, domestic silver at market price. The stockpiles were minted into dollars, which led to such a glut that banks had surplus bags stored in vaults for years after they had been minted. Although the Sherman Act was a boon to Western silver barons, it undermined the nation's economy and, combined with falling farm prices and a drain on gold reserves, helped to plunge the country into a panic in early 1893. While silver prices continued to decline, the bottom fell out when Great Britain announced in

June 1893 that it would no longer mint silver coins from its mines in India, collapsing the worldwide market. President Grover Cleveland, a staunch gold standard advocate, made good on his campaign promise and induced Congress to revoke the Sherman Act in November 1893.[21]

By that time, virtually all silver mining had stopped, and Colorado's economy went into free fall. Fifty per cent of the state's miners were without jobs. People left in droves. The remaining population had scant resources for going to the opera house.[22]

Silver prices bottomed out in the spring of 1894. Although mining would never again rise to its pre-1890 prominence, the business's diversification into manganese, copper, and other metals, as well as the Cripple Creek gold strikes, helped the state's economy to rebound. Still, opulent opera houses struggled to stay open, with varying degrees of success. Some became neglected monuments to the optimism of an earlier time; many were converted into part- or full-time movie houses, but with dwindling populations, even these faced uncertain futures. Over the years, the majority were torn down, burned down, or so thoroughly rebuilt as to be unrecognizable.

Ironically, most of the theatres that survive today are in the small towns hardest hit by the economic downturn at the end of the nineteenth century. The state's largest cities lost almost all their historic theatres to changing neighborhoods, urban renewal, real estate deals, and public apathy. They exist only in photographs, newspaper stories, and the memories of those who patronized them. The remainder stand as symbols of our frontier past, reminders of the importance of their towns in bygone glory days. Most have survived through the heroics of a person or persons who protected them over the years. We are all indebted to these largely unsung heroes, preservers of our ancestors' loftiest dreams.

Many, many small towns in Colorado had opera houses. The Dickens Opera House in Longmont is typical of those that did not have the good fortune to be connected to a railroad circuit that booked theatrical talent. Opened in 1882, the Dickens occupied the second floor of a large, two-story building. It attracted few traveling performers but served as a community center for home talent productions, lectures, amateur concerts, and dances. The Dickens is still standing, is a designated historic landmark, and now houses a bar and billiard parlor.

The theatres described here are representative of those across the state; we have not tried to profile all of them. With one exception, the theatres and opera houses chosen for inclusion in this book were built before 1900. Most were stops on the Silver Circuit, and all were initially constructed to house live theatre, not movies. The restored Sheridan

Opera House in Telluride, for example, is now the home of the annual Telluride Film Festival, which seems appropriate since it was built in 1913 for use primarily as a movie theatre. This tiny, 240-seat house with its restored roll curtain is listed on the National Register of Historic Places.[23] The Mancos Opera House and the Grove Theatre in Alamosa date from the same decade (1910 and 1912, respectively), and both hosted live theatre for about a year before switching to moving pictures. Both are still standing. Because the tenure for live stage productions was so very short, these three theatres are not fully profiled.

Often opera houses built in the late nineteenth-century were subsequently adapted for other uses. Colorado has one instance where the reverse has occurred. The Denver Municipal Auditorium was built in 1908 for the city's use as a large civic arena. Second in size only to Madison Square Garden when it opened, its inaugural event was the National Democratic Convention of 1908. By lowering a proscenium arch across the space, it was possible to use a portion of the building as a theatre, but that was not originally the primary function of the auditorium. With the passage of a bond issue by Denver voters in 2002, the Denver Municipal Auditorium is now being converted into a theatre space, and will include the new Ellie Caulkins Opera House. Slated to open in September 2005, at a total projected cost of $75 million, the Quigg Newton Denver Municipal Auditorium will be home to Opera Colorado, the Denver Brass, the Colorado Ballet, and the Cleo Parker Robinson Dance Ensemble.

Newspaper reviews usually provide the best sources of eyewitness accounts of theatrical productions, and many are quoted here. They are not infallible, however: throughout much of the state's early history, theatre went largely unmarked. Reviews tended to be short, flowery, and descriptive of what occurred on stage rather than the evaluative criticism we expect today. Some early newspapers, archived in small libraries and museums fifty years ago, have simply disappeared, leaving us to rely on the transcriptions of others. For the most part, the authors have chosen to let the reviews speak for themselves.

In the spring of 1996, the authors visited the Colorado History Museum in Denver to see the permanent exhibits chronicling the life of Horace Tabor. Surprisingly, the photograph labeled the Tabor Grand Opera House in the museum's collection was not that high Victorian Gothic building, but instead a photo of the much less striking office building referred to as the Tabor Block. The mix-up serves as a reminder that much of Colorado's rich theatre history is unknown to today's theatregoers and residents. Many of the pictures included in this book have not been widely published, if at all. Little, unaccountably, has been written on several of these glorious theatres. In an age in which the word "theatre" conjures up the anonymous twelve-plex movie house at the nearest mall, Coloradans should remember the grand tradition they have inherited. We hope the following stories and photographs will rekindle interest in the theatres that remain and help us treasure what is left of the state's rich theatrical past.

CHAPTER TWO

CENTRAL CITY

Central City Opera House

OPENED: MARCH 4, 1878

CURRENTLY A SUMMER OPERA HOUSE

The Central City Opera House is the *grand dame* of Colorado's historic theatres. It is the oldest playhouse still operating in Colorado, and with relatively short lapses, it has been used continuously. Unlike a number of its historic companions, it was built by money from gold mining rather than silver. Put up by pioneers without a wealthy patron to foot the bill, it survived the decline of its town through the dedication of a few tenacious souls who recognized its singularity. Remarkably, it thrives today as an internationally recognized home for summer opera, isolated in a mountain town of a few hundred.

Central City grew up near Gregory Gulch, site of the May 1859 gold discovery of John H. Gregory. Gold seekers had been in what was called the Pikes Peak region for about a year, when the first large strike was found by George Jackson on Chicago Creek in January 1859. Working thirty-five miles away, Gregory found gold about five months later. As news of the strike spread, mining hopefuls poured in by the thousands.

The newly platted town of Central City housed 594 residents by the summer of 1860. Rustic theatre arrived not long afterward, presented in a number of halls and featuring everything from variety shows and balls to billiards demonstrations. Jack Langrishe and his pioneer theatrical troupe spent summers in Central City for eighteen years, more time than they spent anywhere outside of Denver. Langrishe owned a home in Central City and was well liked by its townspeople. The Langrishe company produced a variety of entertainments, instilling in Central City residents an appreciation of theatre from the very beginnings of the town and encouraging locals to produce their own amateur theatricals when Langrishe was at his Denver theatre or traveling the territory. Perhaps because of the frequent exposure to good theatre provided by Langrishe, Central City citizens developed a discriminating taste for stage productions. Likewise, in contrast to the normally brief and blandly complimentary newspaper coverage in Leadville and elsewhere, Central City papers usually ran complete, if matter-of-fact, reviews, which were given to unvarnished opinions.

Nevertheless, the veneer of respectability produced by the presence of theatres in what was still a fledgling mining camp was thin. George W. Harrison, manager of the National Theatre, which had opened in 1861, gained notoriety when he shot and killed a sworn enemy, the manager of a newly arrived band of minstrels, from the balcony of a building adjacent to his theatre in July 1862. The murder was judged justifiable, the public reaction was casual, and Harrison continued on as a theatre manager for a number of years.

Such lawlessness was unusual in Central City. As was recalled years later by an early resident:

> *Central City never was quite as tough and turbulent a place as were, for example, Leadville and Creede. There were not so many disreputable resorts as in many other new mining towns, and while there were occasional shooting scrapes, they were rather far apart, considering the fact that adventurers from all parts of the world were attracted by the gold finds. Even our toughs were pretty good fellows.*[1]

Harrison's National Theatre was renamed the Montana in 1862 and served as the principal theatre for Central City until a disastrous fire in 1874 destroyed it, along with much of the rest of the clapboard town. Until the fire, touring groups that reached Denver often included a stop at Central City, allowing townsfolk to see the likes of Milton Nobles and the Christy Minstrels. Although the theatre was not luxurious, it had undergone a number of improvements and enlargements over the years, and its loss was felt severely, as recorded by resident Frank Crissey Young:

Of all the destruction wrought by the fire, I make bold to say there is nothing more keenly regretted as a public loss than that of the Montana Theatre. . . . We carried away with us no memory of the hard seats, or the severely plain auditorium, the bizarre curtain, or the poorly clothed stage. . . . The town indeed must have its theatre, and some day, no doubt, it will build a new one; but . . . I doubt if it can ever be to the future community what the old Montana was.[2]

Despite such sentimentality, efforts quickly commenced to replace the theatre. Central City resident and later U.S. Senator Henry Teller helped finance the construction of a new theatre in the second story of the town's armory in 1875. Called the Belvidere, it was not lavish, but it served the purpose for the increasing number of home talent productions being staged by the town's music-loving residents, including the large number of Cornish, Welsh, and German miners. The Belvidere still stands at the top of Main Street, although it has not been used as a theatre for many years.

Despite some popular performances there, the shortcomings of the Belvidere were obvious. In May 1877, a committee convened to look into the possibility of building an "attractive and elegant" opera house that would present not only local theatricals but also attract touring groups. The Gilpin County Opera House Association set about soliciting contributions from Central City residents and succeeded in raising over $12,000 in short order. Everyone contributed, from the five-dollar donations of miners, to the substantial sums given by Senator Teller and his brother, Willard. Central City proudly claimed its opera house was "Erected by private capital and public subscription."

Having no single, well-heeled benefactor, the Association kept its eye on the bottom line and began planning a sober and restrained building: no imported hardwoods or plush and lace interiors for this opera house. The fluffy Parisian-style building proposed by one resident was rejected in favor of the proposal of Denver architect Robert S. Roeschlaub. Roeschlaub envisioned, in the words of his daughter, Alice, "one that should be in harmony with the great mountains surrounding it, and an expression of the new and simple West."[3]

Built on Eureka Street on the site of a livery stable, the opera house fit that description exactly as it took shape over the next several months. Ground was broken on June 14, 1877, and work proceeded slowly, punctuated by stoppages to raise more money. Roeschlaub chose granite from the surrounding mountains for the facade's massive, four-foot-thick walls. Richard Bretell described the building years later in his *Historic Denver.*

The Central City Opera House is indubitably Roeschlaub's best known building. The austere stone facade gives the smallish building a sobriety and grandness lacking in most buildings of the Second Empire style. Probably for budgetary reasons, Roeschlaub eschewed the opportunity to cover the building in ornament. He divided the facade into three blocky masses, a central area with a mansard roof flanked by doors, and succeeded in giving the building a great deal more solidarity and depth than neighboring street buildings with their implacably flat facades. The Central City Opera House is admirable for its straight-forwardness and simplicity.[4]

An early photo of the Central City Opera House (date unknown). The façade was built of four-foot-thick granite blocks taken from the surrounding mountains.
PHOTO COURTESY DENVER PUBLIC LIBRARY, WESTERN HISTORY COLLECTION, X-11568

Construction was handled by local builders Will and Peter McFarlane; the remainder of the latter's life would be connected to this building. Since the opera house was to have the largest stage in the state, newspapers from throughout Colorado followed the building's progress. Denver's *Rocky Mountain News* reported that it would be "one of the handsomest public edifices in the state" and would have "the most beautiful auditorium to be found between Chicago and San Francisco."[5]

For a town of 3,000, construction of such an imposing building with seating for over seven hundred was news indeed. Central City was giving notice that it intended to be a major player in the state's future.

Although most theatres of the age combined office and retail space with an auditorium in one building, Central City's opera house was designed solely as a theatre. The interior was suitably well appointed, with specially designed folding chairs, known as patent opera seats, for the lower level, two furnaces, and an artfully frescoed ceiling painted by John C. Massman of San Francisco. The center of the ceiling was painted as an "open dome," and the *Rocky Mountain News* reporter suggested it led one to "imagine he is looking through the roof at the sky overhead with angry clouds hurrying by *en route* to Georgetown and Pike's Peak direct without change, as the railroad guides say."[6] In keeping with its democratic origins, there were no boxes, perhaps because there were no principal donors who wished to be seen from them.

The stage and auditorium were lighted by gas, although only three months before the opening, the intention to use a complex kerosene system had been reported in the *Daily Central City Register*. A one-hundred-lamp kerosene chandelier proposed to light the auditorium was not installed; instead a thirty-two-light gas chandelier was mounted. The discrepancy in reporting has led to confusion about the original lighting system, but contemporary newspaper accounts show clearly that gas was used. Complaints about the inadequacy of the stage lighting appeared in reviews several months after the theatre's opening, although they seem to have been rectified by June 1879.

The stage measured 40 feet by 50 feet, with a height from the stage to the riggings of 40 feet. The stage curtain depicted a balcony landscape scene, with the Rhine and a castle in the foreground. Massman also painted seven sets of scenery, including garden, parlor, prison, and forest, providing basic sets for touring companies traveling without their own properties. There were four dressing rooms, which the local reviewer called "elegant." The dress circle and parquet accommodated five hundred, with additional seating for 250 in the gallery. The two sets of stairs rising to the auditorium were so ample, the reviewer concluded, "that the whole audience can walk out almost at once. Taken all in all it is a theatre of which any city might be proud, and is as far superior to anything Denver has or ever had that no comparison need to be instituted."[7]

As with most ambitious building projects, costs quickly outstripped the monies collected by the Association. Late in the construction process, a mortgage in the amount of $6,000 was proposed and accepted, bringing the final cost of the theatre to about $23,000.

Although the opera house was originally intended to open in December 1877, delays pushed back the opening until the following March. Meanwhile, residents considered what would be a

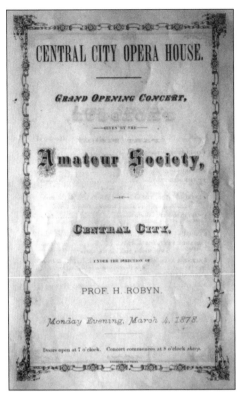

CENTRAL CITY OPERA HOUSE.

GRAND OPENING CONCERT,
—GIVEN BY THE—

Amateur Society,
—OF—
CENTRAL CITY.

UNDER THE DIRECTION OF

PROF. H. ROBYN.

Monday Evening, March 4, 1878.

Doors open at 7 o'clock.   Concert commences at 8 o'clock sharp.

The cover of the opening night program,
Central City Opera House. The opera
house actually had two opening nights, the
first of which, pictured here, featured
operatic excerpts; on the second, a four-act
play and farce were performed.
PHOTO COURTESY DENVER PUBLIC LIBRARY,
WESTERN HISTORY COLLECTION, X-17492

suitable opening-night program. Newspaper articles had announced a home talent production of the opera *Martha* would be given, but some in the community complained. Instead, organizers proposed *two* opening nights, the first musical and the second dramatic, with both featuring members of Central City's own Amateur Society. Advertisements announced that the initial March 4, 1878 performance was to be "a GRAND CONCERT of INSTRUMENTAL and VOCAL MUSIC...[with] operatic choruses, solos, duets, trios, etc." Music was intentionally selected from a variety of nationalities to represent the many immigrants in Central City. Everything was to be sung in English, an intriguing choice, given the Central City Opera Association's decision to do opera entirely in English translation fifty years later.

Anticipating a sellout, Colorado Central added special trains to bring theatregoers from Denver and other cities. The reviewer for Denver's *Rocky Mountain News* reported:

> *The evening train brought an additional and much larger delegation of the hungriest people ever seen in the gulch since the fall of '60. They swarmed into the dining room of the Teller House, and would have bred a famine there, but for the fact that Bush is always prepared for such emergencies, and his larder is never quite exhausted. Supper over, they swarmed up street to the opera house, and the rush for seats was worse than the rush for supper.*[8]

The crowd was wildly appreciative of the performance: The *Daily Register-Call* reported that "[w]hen the curtain was raised for the first time . . . the applause was almost deafening, and it was some minutes before the opening overture could begin."[9] Newspapers enthusiastically reported the gala, down to the colors of the gowns and hair ornaments of the ladies in attendance. Elizabeth McCourt Doe, better known as Baby Doe, saw both opening-night performances with her first husband, Harvey. She would leave Harvey for Leadville and Horace Tabor by the end of the following year.

The thirty-two operatic selections made for a long opening night; patrons left the theatre after 11:00. The next night's offering was longer still. *School*, a popular four-act comedy by T. W. Robertson, was followed by a farce, *Cool as a Cucumber*. The review in Central's *Evening Call* on March 5, 1878, was exultant:

> *If ever the people of Central had reason to feel proud of the energy and enterprise of the first city of the mountains, it was last night upon the opening of her magnificent opera house, which today stands the finest temple of the Muses west of the Missouri, and far ahead of anything of the kind ever projected in the Rocky Mountains.*

Two weeks after the grand opening, the first professional production appeared. *Mazeppa*, the sensational melodrama starring Fannie Louise Buckingham, was presented to a crowded house. Adapted from a Byron poem, the title character in *Mazeppa* is male; however, by the 1870s it had become popular for a woman to play the role. The climactic scene features Mazeppa strapped naked to a wild horse, with rider and steed charging onstage in the portrayal of a headlong run to ruin and death. This spectacular effect was achieved by having the horse run on a stage-mounted treadmill, while a panorama of scenery was rolled behind the horse and rider in the opposite direction. Actresses in the part were also not naked, although scanty costumes suggested it and added considerable interest to the scene.

Miss Buckingham was supported by members of a Colorado troupe managed by Nate C. Forrester. The *Evening Call*'s mixed review noted:

> *Miss Buckingham is a very handsome, well-formed woman, who certainly looks the character of "Mazeppa," if her acting does not in every particular come up to the usual standard. Her horsemanship is superb, if her elocution and gestures, in some instances are faulty. But*

artistes in her line are never expected to be perfect in elocution. . . .
People do not go to listen to finished declamation, but to see
"Mazeppa," and the impartial amusement lover is always inclined
to overlook such shortcomings in the magnificent form and physque
[sic] of the actress.[10]

Forrester's troupe remained in the city for some time, acting as a stock company in support of stars who were touring the Rockies. Forrester booked a variety of companies into the Central City Opera House in addition to his own, including minstrel and variety shows. On average, touring groups appeared every two or three weeks, interspersed with local programs and meetings. Quality performances were not always the order of the day, as when adaptations of Jules Verne's novels were given by a California company. "Flat fraud," the reviewer declared, stating they were undeserving of the large audience they drew. Still, audiences responded warmly to the pianist known as Blind Tom and to engagements by the Forresters. For a small, isolated town used to relying on its own resources for entertainment, the changes brought by the construction of the opera house must have seemed wonderful.

The first of several female "leg shows" played the opera house in January 1879 when The British Blondes came to town. The reviewer noted that those looking for lascivious entertainment were disappointed, opining dryly that "[t]he Ezeltine Sisters are excellent in their specialties, club swinging, while Miss Lottie Elliott is fine as a skipping rope dancer."[11] Perhaps those interested in earthier fare were better pleased when Madame Rentz's Minstrels teamed up with Mabel Santley's Burlesque Company the following June, promising "the Voluptuous Living Art Pictures, the loveliest formed women in the world, The Genuine Parisian Jardin Mabille Can-Can!"[12] The reviewer sniped, "The Female Minstrels gave the can-can in all its deformity and hideousness last night. It is hoped the morbid tastes of boys were satisfied."[13]

Kate Claxton appeared in her signature role in the melodramatic and highly popular *The Two Orphans* the same month to the largest audience since the theatre's opening. Claxton played blind Louise, hapless orphan and companion of the lone and winsome Henriette. Both fend for themselves on the streets of Paris, where Louise is forced to beg for a living by the evil La Frochard, before she is discovered to be propertied and upper class at the end of the play. Brisk ticket sales may have been caused by the notoriety of Miss Claxton in the part, since only three years earlier hundreds had died in a fire during a performance of the play in New York's Brooklyn Theatre. Miss Claxton narrowly escaped death in that tragedy; two other actors were not so fortunate. Tickets to the Central City performance were so sought after that Miss Claxton returned in 1881 to repeat her triumph.

In July 1879, one of the age's leading men, tragedian Lawrence Barrett, appeared to high acclaim, although his single performance brought to a boil a brouhaha that had been simmering between the local newspaper and impresario Forrester, whose troupe had supported Barrett. The altercation began when Forrester failed to pay his advertising bills with the *Daily Register-Call* and escalated when he bounced checks around town, raised prices at the opera house, and treated

Miss KATE CLAXTON, as Louise, in the "Two Orphans."
680 BROADWAY, N. Y.

Kate Claxton (1850-1924) as Louise in
The Two Orphans (date unknown).
COURTESY OF THE HUNTINGTON LIBRARY,
SAN MARINO, CALIFORNIA

visiting stars badly. The paper accused Forrester of fobbing off second-rate groups onto Central; Forrester countered by announcing his disinclination to return his stock company to Central. The paper drew a line in the sand, stating, "Neither Mr. Forrester nor any entertainment under his management need look for any courtesy from this office until he has settled up his indebtedness and explained away his very uncourteous conduct in his dealings with us."[14]

By December of 1879, a troupe more to Central's liking than Forrester's appeared for the first time at the opera house. The Plunkett family performed five plays in a week and over the years came as close as any to filling the void left by the well-loved Langrishe company. Jack Langrishe, in fact, had made his last appearance in Central only the month before. He drifted in and out of Colorado for several years before finally settling down for the last ten years of his life in Warner, Idaho.

For a brief time, theatre flourished in bustling Central City. When the railroad arrived from nearby Black Hawk two months after the opening of the opera house, residents must have felt certain of a vigorous future. The presence of this jewel of a theatre represented a pinnacle in the history of the "little kingdom of Gilpin." But at almost the same time Central City reached its apex, other forces were at hand that would lead to its decline.

The killjoy was silver. After its discovery in Leadville and elsewhere, fortune-seekers turned their attention from Central's waning gold deposits to the fabulous riches to be had from the seemingly plentiful ore. The population at Central peaked and began to fall. Attendance at the opera house suffered, a situation aggravated by the opening in Denver of the Tabor Grand Opera House in September 1881, which effectively eclipsed the much plainer Central City Opera House.

Not all the consequences of the discovery of silver were bad. With the increased number of theatres in the area, some troupes that might never have been enticed to come otherwise made the trip to Colorado, stopping in Central City along the way. The development of the Silver Circuit allowed residents of Central City to see some of the biggest names in theatre, albeit for one-night stands. Madame Janauschek came in January 1880 and was hailed as "magnificently grand," prompting the audience to "h[a]ng in breathless suspense upon every syllable that fell from her lips."[15]

Not everyone recognized greatness when it came, as the *Daily Register-Call* reviewer pointedly reminded readers who had missed William E. Sheridan and Rose Keene and Company in June 1881:

> *We certainly fail to appreciate the taste which fills the house to see Haverly's New Mastodons (which by the way are not even excellent of their kind) and fails to attend the performance of one of the brightest stars upon the stage anywhere. Theater goers will wait a long time before they have an opportunity to see the equal of the productions of last night and night before.*[16]

Almost twenty troupes stopped in Central City during the 1881–82 season, about the same number that visited Georgetown, and half that of booming Leadville. Attractions were varied, with Shakespeare appearing almost as often as vaudeville and variety shows. However, dwindling audiences brought an end to Central City's glory days, and just four years after it opened, the opera house was put up for sale. The county commissioners agreed to buy it, but they ran into opposition when they announced plans to turn it into a courthouse. Public outcry was loud and organized, and in the end, the commissioners relented, selling the building to the resurrected Gilpin County Opera House Association for roughly the $8,000 they had paid for it.

The new opera house manager was school principal and amateur performer Horace M. Hale. Local groups were encouraged to use the theatre, and some rudimentary renovations were undertaken. A touring production of Boucicault's popular *The Octoroon* was well received. The reviewer wrote, "Dion Boucicault's notion of an Indian don't fit the western idea, but Wah-no-tee [J. J. Lodge] impressed the applause, sympathy and even tears of the audience. Miss Bernard's Dora was so well played that we are at a loss to understand why even the Indian did not fall in love with her."[17] Along with appearances by minstrel groups, lecturers, and local amateurs, John L. Sullivan demonstrated boxing on the stage in 1883. But by the middle of the decade, big-name stars largely bypassed Central City, and Hale and the Association were unable to turn the theatre around financially. When his lease ran out, Hale asked one of the original builders of the opera house, Peter McFarlane, to take over the management.

An unidentified stock company onstage during the Central City Opera House's first decade.
PHOTO COURTESY DENVER PUBLIC LIBRARY, WESTERN HISTORY COLLECTION, X-6032

It was a providential move. McFarlane was a prominent citizen in Central City, owner of a thriving mining supply business and developer of specialized equipment for extracting gold from low-grade ores. He had been Central City's mayor about the time the opera house opened, and over the years his ever-increasing commitment to the theatre was just short of heroic, costing him dearly in time, money, and vexation. As the fortunes of the town declined, so did McFarlane's. Most years the opera house lost money. By the beginning of the 1890s, the Opera House Association was unable to pay its taxes. Bookings dwindled until by 1893, not a single theatre troupe was booked into the opera house. Nonetheless, at his own expense, McFarlane resolutely saw to the repair of the building, beginning with its water-logged basement and leaky roof. In 1896 he installed electric lights.

A flicker of renewal came to Central after the market for silver evaporated in the wake of the repeal of the Sherman Silver Act and gold prices began to go up. Gradually, theatre returned to Central City, although not to the extent of its early triumphs. Central was able to attract Otis Skinner, one of the stage's leading actors, for one performance in February 1900. The review was highly complimentary, even though the house was less full than for the various vaudeville acts that more commonly appeared there. Hypnotists, prize fighters, minstrel shows, and lecturers filled out the bill after 1900.

Increasingly involved in the day-to-day running of the theatre, McFarlane began buying up stock in the Gilpin County Opera Association, and by 1901 he was majority shareholder, a position he retained until his death almost thirty years later. In a letter to Henry Teller reflecting on his decision to control the opera house, McFarlane wrote, "I've only regretted it once, and that is all the time."[18] Over the years, McFarlane doggedly continued to work on his theatre. In 1903, he almost single-handedly began a renovation, the most significant part of which was the replacement of the original patent opera seats with no-nonsense hickory kitchen chairs, whose unyielding frames tortured the backsides of theatregoers for decades.

Always seeking a way to make his theatre pay, McFarlane successfully petitioned the city council to allow Sunday theatricals, permitting him to book attractions that had played in Denver on Saturday night. Though not all his bookings were quality nor his houses full, Sunday performances kept the theatre open through the early years of the century. By the end of the decade, though, the number of bookings began to fall again: in 1907, there were more than twenty bookings; two years later, only three were scheduled. McFarlane was disgusted with the quality of the offerings available to him and complained to Silver Circuit manager Peter McCourt in a letter, "It's not pleasant to be pointed at by the finger of scorn because of a bum show and bum occurs to be the only word this season."[19]

In 1910 McFarlane installed a projection camera, hoping to capitalize on the popularity of films. He was successful enough that the theatre did not close, but most years it still lost money. No doubt part of the reason was the personality of the owner himself: he was known to let hoards of children into the theatre to see popular films free. A moral man, he was indignant when films violated his sense of propriety for children's viewing. Love stories exasperated him. In a letter to his supplier, he claimed, not altogether accurately, "The manufacturers will have to come up with something else besides *love* and *hugging* all the time. The public is getting tired of too much kissing."[20] McFarlane also had a penchant for booking touring groups he wanted to see, especially if they were doing Shakespeare. He let out the

Peter McFarlane (1848-1929), one of the original builders of the Central City Opera House, was called by his biographer "the Little Kingdom's most loyal citizen" (date unknown).
AMERICAN HERITAGE CENTER, UNIVERSITY OF WYOMING, NEG. 21910

building for graduation exercises and other local, but unprofitable, productions until after the end of the First World War. Live companies came sporadically, and finally not at all. The last professional group to appear on the stage of the opera house during McFarlane's long tenure was the Colonial Singers in the summer of 1919.

Later that year, McFarlane summed up the situation of Central City and its struggling opera house: "Five % of our people died, 10% are in mourning, 25% have moved away, 35% are penniless, 15% out of employment, leaving 10% only to support amusements."[21] McFarlane bowed to the inevitable and closed his opera house on New Year's Day 1927, having kept the place afloat against very long odds for over thirty years. He died two years later, without seeing the renewal he had always expected for the beloved town he called home for sixty years.

Ida Kruse McFarlane (1884-
1940), daughter-in-law of
Peter McFarlane, in 1921.
COURTESY OF CENTRAL
CITY OPERA

Unwittingly, he helped inspire it.
Although the opera house was ostensibly owned by the Gilpin County Opera
Association, McFarlane's three children
had inherited eighty per cent of its
stock. Property tax payment was several
years in arrears, and thought was given
to converting the building to a gymnasium or garage after paying the delin-
quent tax bill. Into the discussion
stepped Ida Kruse McFarlane, Peter's
daughter-in-law. Several versions are
told of what transpired, but apparently
Ida, working in conjunction with
Denver Civic Theatre's director Walter
Sinclair, conceived the idea of restoring
the opera house and using it as the home
for a summer dramatic festival. The
McFarlane heirs—Frederick, George,
and Yetta—agreed. They acquired clear
title to the opera house, paid the back
taxes, and, in 1932, donated the theatre
to the University of Denver.

The third principal in the rescue of the opera house now appeared,
along with Peter McFarlane and his daughter-in-law. Anne Evans was a
community arts activist and daughter of Colorado's second territorial
governor. A member of the board charged by the University of Denver
with deciding whether or not to accept the McFarlane gift, Anne Evans
went to work raising money to repair the dank, rat-infested theatre and
making it habitable for performances. Her most original and visible idea
was to sell inscriptions for $100 apiece for each of the old, straight-
backed chairs installed by Peter McFarlane decades earlier, recording on
each the name of a Colorado pioneer and the date he or she arrived in
Colorado. Among those memorialized were the opera house's architect,
Robert Roeschlaub, kindhearted former slave and early Central City
resident "Aunt Clara" Brown, and, of course, Peter McFarlane.

To begin a dramatic festival anywhere in Depression-era America
was most unpromising, but the odds were very long against setting one
in a remote, tattered mining town of 500 in the mountains of Colorado
in 1932. The founders of the Central City Opera House Association,
which included Miss Evans, Mrs. McFarlane, and muralist Allen True,
proceeded to engage one of Broadway's leading lights, Robert Edmond

The turn-of-the-century hickory chair inscribed for Peter McFarlane prior to the 1932 Central City Festival.
PHOTO COURTESY DENVER PUBLIC LIBRARY, WESTERN HISTORY COLLECTION, X-6020

Jones, to direct the first festival. Jones rejected the early proposal to stage a traditional melodrama. He wisely asserted, "To revive an old play for the amusement in it seemed to cheapen the theatre, to be unfitting. The building simply stood there and, in spite of its grime and neglect, it imposed an obligation, delivered a challenge either to let it alone or to do something worthy within it."[22] Eventually, he decided to produce *Camille*, engaging Lillian Gish for the principal role. It was the first of many startlingly unexpected appearances by renowned theater people who made their way to Central.

Such an audacious start made headlines, and as the opening approached, newspapers and magazines from the *New York Times* to *Vanity Fair* and *Theatre Arts Monthly* sent reporters to cover it. The NBC radio network

The Central City Opera House as it appeared in 1933, a year after its rebirth. The original mansard roof has been replaced and the musician's balcony rebuilt.
PHOTO COURTESY DENVER PUBLIC LIBRARY, WESTERN HISTORY COLLECTION, LAURA GILPIN, X-11563

Central City's stage, curtain, and some of John Massman's elaborate ceiling frescoes, after their restoration in 1932 by muralist Allen True.

The auditorium of the Central City Opera House, c. 1932. The damage to the walls is apparent, although the turn-of-the-century hickory chairs look sturdy.

The wooden playbill at the Central City Opera House announcing the first festival in 1932. Similar playbills have announced each production ever since.
PHOTO COURTESY DENVER PUBLIC LIBRARY, WESTERN HISTORY COLLECTION

Crowds on opening night, 1932, for the newly renovated Central City Opera House.
PHOTO COURTESY DENVER PUBLIC LIBRARY, WESTERN HISTORY COLLECTION, HARRY M. RHOADS, RH-387

Curtain call for Lillian
Gish after her opening
night performance in
Camille, 1932.
COURTESY OF CENTRAL
CITY OPERA

did a live broadcast of the July 16, 1932 opening ceremonies. Central City decked itself out accordingly, stocking storefront windows with merchandise from the 1870s and transporting guests in a variety of hackneys, carriages, and other horse-drawn conveyances. Theatregoers were asked to dress in period costume. In a nod to Central's pioneer antecedents, Jack Langrishe III appeared on stage in honor of his illustrious ancestor. The production was an unqualified success. Reviewers were struck by the evocation of a distant era as they sat, surrounded by an audience wearing nineteenth-century silk hats and gloves, seeing a period play performed in a theatre from the same age. The *Chicago News* reviewer declared Miss Gish's performance "moving, finished, unforgettable." He concluded, "As we drove back . . . we felt that for this memorable night at least, we were the darlings of the gods."[23]

The second season moved from drama to operetta, with Gladys Swarthout and Richard Bonelli appearing in *The Merry Widow*. Lavish international press attention, most of it highly complimentary, accompanied the production. Switching back to drama for the 1934 season, Robert Edmond Jones invited his brother-in-law, Walter Huston, to abandon his $3,000-a-week Broadway role in *Dodsworth* to appear with his wife, Nan Sunderland, in a Central City production of *Othello* for a total salary of $1,000. "Dear Bobby," came Huston's reply. "Your terms are entirely unsatisfactory; I accept."[24]

Having attracted attention from around the country, the fledgling festival built on its successes, with opera gradually replacing drama as the season's focus. Directorial control went from Robert Edmond Jones to Frank St. Leger. The latter championed the practice of performing opera in English, a stand eventually supported by the Association and in effect until 2000, when the decision was made to perform all operas in their original language. The reviewer for the *Dallas Times* expressed the pleasure of many when he wrote of a 1941 production, "*The Barber of Seville* turns out to be a riotous comedy when given in the vernacular by artists who know how to enunciate. While the musical elements are not neglected, this opera is played with the brilliant farce that it is."[25]

The new festival had its share of difficulties. Ida Kruse McFarlane and Anne Evans died within a year of each other, in 1940 and early 1941, respectively. The theatre was dark from 1942 to 1945, as the energies and resources of the country went to the war effort. Still, the festival was resurrected in 1946 and took up where it had left off. Under the guidance of Frank Ricketson, who served as president of the Association from 1941 to 1964, two operas were produced each summer. In 1947, a play was added to the end of the season with a New York cast, capitalizing on Broadway's tradition of closing in August. Coloradan Mary Chase's *Harvey* was the first, establishing a pattern of good receipts from the season-closing play, which helped to compensate for the always expensive opera productions. Mae West appeared flamboyantly in *Diamond Lil* in 1949, throwing herself a birthday party in Central City with an all-male guest list and installing mirrors on the ceiling of her cottage.

Central City's productions continued to draw praise. Composer and critic Virgil Thomson wrote in 1948 that the opera house had "an acoustical liveliness . . . that is not equalled by more than a half a dozen houses of its kind in the world. . . . For general musical excellence, the performances were the equal of any opera performances available anywhere today and far, far better than many produced in more pretentious circumstances."[26]

The 1950s saw productions of well-known operas coupled with rarely performed ones, such as Suppé's *The Beautiful Galatea* and Strauss's *Ariadne auf Naxos*. In 1956, the Central City Opera House Association went a step further, commemorating its colorful past by sponsoring an original opera based on Colorado history. The Koussevitzky Foundation commissioned the work, which was composed by Douglas Moore with a libretto by John Latouche. The plot was based on the stories of Colorado's Silver King, Horace Tabor, and his wives, Augusta and Baby Doe. Despite difficulties with the libretto, *The Ballad of Baby Doe* was presented at the Central City Opera House on July 7, 1956. The *New York Journal American* proclaimed it "the most authentic American opera yet produced in this country."[27] J. S. Harrison, writing for the *New York Herald Tribune,* praised its musicality:

> *Douglas Moore and John Latouche have . . . given us the West in ringing song. . . . The airs are all floated on an ingenious and easily accessible orchestral base and even the recitative has a willowy suppleness to make it communicate with pace and power.*[28]

Although there have been other attempts by the Central City Opera House Association at original productions drawn on Colorado history, *The Ballad of Baby Doe* is the only one to achieve a permanent place in the repertory.

A scene from the original 1956 production of ***The Ballad of Baby Doe*** at the Central City Opera Festival. The real Baby Doe left Central City in 1879 for Leadville, where the opera's story begins—outside the Tabor Opera House.
PHOTO COURTESY COLORADO HISTORICAL SOCIETY, F38268

As years passed, the national and international press paid less attention to the season in Central City, while local theatregoers paid more. For decades the year-end fund balances were marginal, with profits or losses of a few hundred dollars, although attendance was generally high. A good season would be followed by a bad one, or attendance would be held down by inexplicable drops in ticket sales, hikes in gas prices, or bad reviews. Sometimes the operas were good, but fundraising was down. Frank Ricketson insisted on financial stability, which was accomplished through expanded programs, increased real estate holdings, and cautious programming.

After experimenting with producing three operas and a play each season in the mid-60s, the Association retrenched to a two-opera, one-play format in 1969. Financial difficulties mounted, and in 1971 it was announced there would be no opera season at all. Serious thought was given to eliminating opera altogether in Central City and performing it instead in Denver. Eventually the opera season survived, with a laudable but risky commitment to stage a contemporary or little-known opera each year.

In 1978, the centenary year of the opera house, *The Bohemian Girl* was chosen to commemorate the production of one hundred years earlier. John Moriarty arrived that same year to conduct the other opera, *Don Pasquale*. He was promoted to principal conductor and artistic director in 1983, a position he retained until 1998. His tenure marked a shift in direction toward ensemble companies and away from big-name opera stars. The Apprentice Artist program flourished under his tenure and has become a sought-after way for young singers to gain experience in everything from diction to stage movement to acting. Mr. Moriarty listened to about a thousand audition tapes each year from applicants vying for fewer than thirty openings as understudies and chorus members.

The late 1970s and early 1980s were stressful years for the Association, as the debt continued to grow and imperiled grant money. Broadway theatres ceased closing in August, thereby ending the Central City festival's practice of importing a packaged moneymaker to close the season. Because of serious financial difficulties, the fiftieth anniversary season in 1982 was canceled and a major reorganization was undertaken. Properties owned by the Association were sold to balance the books, and the Association moved to a season of two standard repertory operas and an operetta. These and other changes turned the tide: since 1982, seasons have usually been profitable and the house is often sold out. Needed renovations have been made, including re-creation of Massman's ceiling frescoes, first refurbished by Allen True in 1932.

Over the years, some of the brightest stars in the opera firmament have sung at Central City, including Paul Plishka, Catherine Malfitano, and Beverly Sills. Critics noted Jerome Hines's appearance in 1948 in *The Tales of Hoffman*, prior to his rise to stardom at the Met. Others got their start there as young singers. Samuel Ramey sang in the chorus of *Don Giovanni* in 1963, his first experience performing opera; he watched

Sherrill Milnes sing the role of Masetto. Plishka remarked, "I would think that just about every . . . American opera singer who comes to the Metropolitan Opera today has at one point gone to Central City."[29]

Gambling has had an off-again, on-again history in Central City from the time the festival opened in 1932. Though gambling was never strictly legal, enforcement agencies alternately winked and cracked down on the presence of games of chance and slot machines. With the passage of limited stakes gambling legislation in 1991, the character of Central City has changed, with mixed results for the Opera House Association. Expenses have risen and ticket sales have dropped, although the percentage of seats sold has rebounded since the 1991 season. On a more positive note, city and state gambling proceeds have financed extensive restoration of the opera house, its auxiliary buildings, and the Association-owned Victorian homes that house cast and crew members. The restoration money has allowed fundraising efforts to be concentrated on a rehearsal complex, fittingly built on the site of Peter and Will McFarlane's foundry. The opening of the Central City Parkway in November 2004 improves access for patrons of the opera house and the town from I-70.

The Central City Opera House Association is the oldest performing arts organization in the state, and across the country, there are only a handful of opera festivals that have operated longer. Its historic home, now 120 years old, and nestled in a town redolent with early Colorado history, is a remarkable institution. Built with frontier optimism, the opera house survived boom, bust, depression, and decay to emerge as one of the state's principal heirlooms. Association co-founder Anne Evans predicted in 1940, "Someday Central City will become a living shrine to living theatre and the early pioneers of Colorado."[30] With its extensive outreach education and training programs for young artists, active guild, and summer-long season, it has certainly succeeded while remaining, in the words of the festival's first director, Robert Edmond Jones, "the most enchanting theatre in America."

CHAPTER THREE

DENVER

Tabor Grand Opera House

OPENED: SEPTEMBER 5, 1881

CONVERTED TO A MOVIE THEATRE: 1921

DEMOLISHED: OCTOBER 1964

In its early days, Denver shared the characteristics of both a mining boomtown and growing commercial center. Its population increased dramatically after gold was discovered in the South Platte River and the town was founded in 1858. Of its early inhabitants, one miner wrote in 1859, "Certainly a more reckless, unprincipled set of men never got together in one place than here."[1] At the same time, theatre established an early foothold at the Apollo Hall, located on the second floor of the Apollo Saloon on Larimer Street, where *Cross of Gold* was first performed on October 3, 1859, by a traveling company led by Colonel C. R. Thorne. Candlelit, without plaster or ceiling, this theatre "seat[ed] any three hundred and fifty willing to pay $1. in gold dust to sit huddled upon its wooden benches." In this setting, plays could often not be heard because of singing from the saloon below, and rowdies interrupted performances with "indecent and riotous exhibitions." But there were compensations: the actors would sometimes be invited downstairs for a drink between acts, and spectators practiced the charming custom of throwing bags of gold dust on the stage as a sign of approval.[2]

The real history of theatre in Denver began with the arrival of Jack Langrishe and his company at the Apollo on September 25, 1860. A proposed six-day engagement extended to eleven years, as Langrishe (with his business partner, M. J. Dougherty) first remodeled and renamed the Apollo the "People's Theatre" on November 30, 1861. Then on October 18, 1862, he opened the Denver Theatre, which remained the town's leading playhouse until it burned in March 1877, presenting "rich, racy and refreshing Songs, Dances, Gags, Local Allusions and Pikes Peak Perpetrations."[3] The theatre looked something like a barn on the outside, but the interior featured an inclined stage, plastered walls, gilded woodwork, and an auditorium that could seat 1,500. During seasons lasting typically from October to April with few interruptions, the Langrishe company offered a huge repertory, featuring everything from Shakespeare (*Othello* being a particular favorite) and melodrama to popular plays like *Uncle Tom's Cabin, The Octoroon, The Lady of Lyons,* and adaptations of Scott's and Dickens's novels. Just as important, Langrishe established rules of decorum in his theatre. No swearing was allowed, the company did not perform on Sundays, and Langrishe offered a monthly benefit for Denver's poor relief fund. These practices brought an air of gentility to Denver theatre for the first time and enticed ladies and Denver society, what there was of it, to patronize the performances. Seldom were shows interrupted by audience members talking and laughing or by the impromptu participation during *La Tour de Nesle* in October 1860:

> *A few persons in the audience added to the amusement of the listeners, especially one who rose during a most thrilling scene, where Walter frantically inquires for his brother, and in a voice which trembled as if seriously affected by Western Whiskey, solemnly ejaculated, "I am thy brother." A roar of laughter greeted the voluntary "supe[rnumerary]."*[4]

Despite tremendous personal popularity, Langrishe fell victim to a declining economy and competition from the earthier variety theatres in the 1870s, and he resorted to touring for much of his remaining career. His position as leader of Denver's theatre was eclipsed by the enthusiasm and investments of Horace Tabor, one of the state's richest men, who was elected in 1878 as its lieutenant governor. When Tabor moved to Denver from Leadville in 1880, he did not leave behind his sense of civic responsibility and desire to erect new buildings in a city now with 34,629 residents. Having recently completed the Tabor Block, a large office building designed by the well-known Chicago architect William J. Edbrooke, Tabor wished to construct a truly grand opera house that would far surpass his own Tabor Opera House in Leadville in both expense and stature. He began in March 1880 by purchasing lots at the corner of Curtis and

Sixteenth Streets for $57,000, then hired Edbrooke to design the building (with his partner, F. P. Burnham) and travel with him back East for three weeks to visit theatres and gather ideas for his own. Construction of the opera house block began in May 1880.

Visiting the building site with his friend, Judge Wilbur Stone, Tabor confided his reasons for financing such a project:

> *I am going to have it just as nice and beautiful as I can have it, for money. I do not intend to cut anything short, for want of money, but you are very much mistaken if you think I am building this other than as a business enterprise; the public may look at it in that way, but I can say to you that I am building this for myself, to make money.*[5]

Tabor was true to his word, and money was no object as he bought trainloads of timbers, iron, and stone for the exterior, as well as carpets, tapestries, chairs, silk plush, mirrors, and carved woodwork for the interior. Eventually the cost would reach $850,000, making the Tabor by far the most expensive theatre in Colorado, and the most lavish. Except for one setback when the north wall collapsed on January 13, 1881, injuring no one but costing $5,000 and thirty extra days of construction, the building steadily took shape and excited the interest of Denverites.[6]

The opera house itself stood five stories tall on a space 75 feet wide and 150 feet deep. The arched entryway from Sixteenth Street was suitably grand, flanked by marble columns with capitals of carved flowers, leaves, and musical emblems. Overhead "The Tabor Grand Opera House" was cut in relief, and higher still, the owner's name appeared. A marble entrance led to a softly lit rotunda, which contained the box office, then to the foyer of the parquet. A splendid, gaslit chandelier illuminated the broad, crimson-carpeted stairways, the lovely cherry-wood newel posts and balustrades, two huge mirrors, and two large panel paintings on either side of the entrance to the parquet—one of the *Fleur de Lis*, the other of sunflowers.[7]

Even this ornate setting gave little hint of what lay on the other side of the heavy curtain separating the foyer from the auditorium. As an early visitor wrote, "The first impression one has is that he has been suddenly transported to some enchanted scene."[8] Edbrooke had designed the theatre in what was called the "Modified Egyptian Moresque" style, a description which hints at its exotic and fantastic qualities. Most striking and innovative of all were the three formal boxes, arranged vertically on each side of the stage, which rose

Exterior of the Tabor Grand Opera House in Denver, c. 1881. The entrance to
the opera house was through the arched portico in the lower right.

"pagoda-like" to within twenty feet of the ceiling and were covered by
a roof resembling a Turkish mosque. Not only were the boxes exceptionally ornate, with their delicate cherry woodwork, thick carpets,
Bourbon tapestries, and silk plush curtains of sage green, maroon, and
gold, but by being set back from the proscenium a short distance, they
afforded a full view of the stage. Next to these "closed" boxes was a similar but less formal set of open or "fashion" boxes, which bordered both
the family circle and the balcony, or "amphitheatre." With the balconies
extended only this far and not wrapped to the proscenium, the theatre
reduced its seating capacity but greatly improved the sightlines and
acoustics for its occupants. Even so, the Tabor was one of the largest
opera houses in the state's history, with a potential capacity of 1,500
divided between the parquet and dress circle (700), family circle (300),
balcony (350), and boxes, in an auditorium measuring 71 feet in width
and 90 feet in length.[9]

The spectacular interior of the Tabor Grand Opera House, c. 1881. Next to the stage are three formal boxes designed in "Modified Egyptian Moresque" style, with a less formal set of open or "fashion" boxes beside them.

PHOTO COURTESY COLORADO HISTORICAL SOCIETY, F369

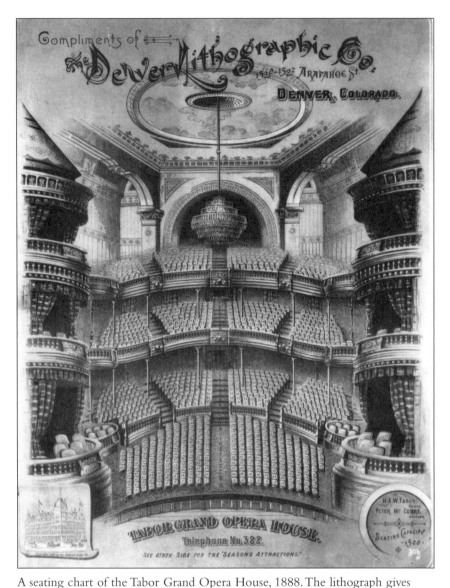

A seating chart of the Tabor Grand Opera House, 1888. The lithograph gives some idea of the theatre's sumptuous beauty.

PHOTO COURTESY COLORADO HISTORICAL SOCIETY, WPA 306

Theatregoers beheld an intricately decorated proscenium arch, 34 feet square, flanked by double columns of polished cherry wood, and surmounted by a semicircular oil painting entitled "Hector's Adieu to Andromaque," by the artist Robert Hopkins. He also painted the complementary drop curtain with its scene of magnificent but decaying architecture, lovely sky, and the words of the poet Kingsley inscribed below:

So fleet the works of men
Back to the earth again—
Ancient and holy things fade like a dream.[10]

In later years when the Tabor was in decline, these verses were often cited as an ironic prophecy of its fate, but such thoughts were far from anyone's mind in 1881. Instead, what most impressed one early viewer was the "richness about everything that one must examine and realize before he can appreciate. Governor Tabor might have saved $30,000 by using cheap woods in the interior construction of the opera house, in the place of the highly polished and carved cherry which is to be found in all parts of the building, even where it will never be seen, unless one takes the trouble to peer into nooks to look for it."[11] But certainly everyone appreciated the more obvious attractions of the crystal and brass chandelier hanging 28 feet from the painted dome, the large circular stained-glass window on the right side of the auditorium, the crimson velvet plush seats, and the imported tapestries.

In keeping with the rest of the theatre, the stage was thoroughly modern and well equipped. It lay 45 feet deep and 72 feet wide, with an ample 19 feet on either side for scene shifting. The 63 feet from the stage to the rigging loft allowed the drop scenes to be raised and lowered easily. Perhaps most notable was the number of painted scenes. At a time when most opera houses were equipped with four standard sets—front room, back room, timber, and town—the Tabor had no less than twenty-four sets, all freshly painted by Hopkins and able to be combined in various ways for optimal utility.[12]

This was the theatre, the fanciest and most famous opera house in Colorado's history and one of the most renowned in the country, that greeted opening-night playgoers on September 5, 1881. The rainy weather did not deter the elite of Denver's society nor those parties that had traveled from as far as Salt Lake City and Kansas City.

Singer Emma Abbott (1850-1891), whose opera company opened the Tabor Grand, 1882.
REPRINTED FROM EMMA ABBOTT GRAND ENGLISH OPERA CO. : KING FOR A DAY, (NEW YORK, 1882). PEORIA PUBLIC LIBRARY

The proscenium arch and drop curtain of the Tabor Grand Opera House (date unknown) surmounted by a semicircular oil painting entitled "Hector's Adieu to Andromaque," by Robert Hopkins. The curtain, displaying Classical ruins, was also by Hopkins.

Neither did the prices—$2.00 for the parquet and dress circle, $1.50 for the family circle, and $1.00 for the balcony—prevent all 1,500 seats from being sold, with a hundred extra seats being added to the aisles and every available niche, and many more requests for tickets turned away.[13] Emma Abbott, the "greatest of Prima Donnas," and her Grand English Opera Company were deemed worthy to open the Tabor Grand in *Maritana*; indeed, inaugurating opera houses was something of an Abbott specialty in the 1880s, with over twenty theatres selecting her for that honor. In recognition of the festive occasion, she preceded her performance in *Maritana* with the famous mad scene from *Lucia de Lammermoor*. Immediately following this popular piece, Tabor was asked to come forward. Because of his recent separation from his wife, Augusta (who had begged in vain to accompany him to the opening), Tabor was not sitting in his private box to the left of the stage, decorated for the occasion with flowers spelling out his name. But he did appear nervously on the stage, endured eulogies and a poem written for the occasion, and received an autographed album and a massive, solid-gold watch fob, which today is on display in the Colorado History Museum along with the souvenir opening-night program. Finally he addressed the expectant audience:

> *It is sixteen months since I commenced the building of this opera house. At that time I looked Denver carefully over with its people and here found a town at the base of the Rocky Mountains—a city of 30,000 or 40,000 inhabitants: the finest city, I think, of its population on the American continent. I said if Denver is to have an opera house it should be worthy of the city. Here is the opera house, I shall leave it to your judgment if I have done my duty in this respect.*[14]

After tumultuous applause, Tabor added his thanks for the gifts, saying, "Here is this beautiful album and fob chain—as beautiful as can be. I shall prize them every hour I live. I shall prize them not for their price value, but for the spirit in which they are given."[15] The evening then proceeded with the scheduled performance of *Maritana*, which was acclaimed with two curtain calls. The *Rocky Mountain News* called the evening "the grandest milestone in Denver's career."[16]

Eugene Field, recently appointed managing editor of the *Denver Tribune*, probably invented the much-repeated story of Tabor who, upon seeing a portrait of Shakespeare in the opera house, ordered that it be replaced by one of himself, adding, "What the hell has he ever done for Colorado?" Field commemorated the opening night with a characteristic piece of verse:

> *The opera house—a union grand*
> *of capital and labor—*
> *Long will the stately structure stand*
> *A monument to Tabor!*[17]

The Abbott Company stayed two weeks, performing several operas and drawing receipts of $27,620, with the theatre clearing a profit of over $7,000. Hearing that the company would proceed to Omaha for two nights, then possibly to Kansas City, Field wrote, "It's a pleasant commentary upon the comparative culture of the so-called rival cities—opera two weeks in Denver, two nights in Omaha, and one matinee in Kansas City."[18]

For the next ten years, the Tabor Grand dominated the Denver theatrical scene and built its reputation as one of the great opera houses in the country. It hosted many theatrical stars from the United States and overseas, including Sarah Bernhardt, Tommaso Salvini, Joseph Jefferson, Rose Eytinge, even Jack Langrishe himself—but not Henry

Irving, the leading Shakespearean actor in England, who never appeared in Denver, contrary to later remembrances. Beginning in May 1882, Lawrence Barrett established himself as a particular favorite with Denver audiences in his repertory of Hamlet, Shylock, Cassius, Richelieu (from Bulwer-Lytton's drama of that name), and other characters. Barrett once told a Denver interviewer, "You have no idea how good it seems to be in a nice clean city where there are sunny weather, a splendid theater to play in and an appreciative audience to play to."[19] An extant treasurer's report shows that a week of Barrett's performances (May 15-20, 1882) produced receipts totaling $7,582.75, with a profit for the Tabor Grand of $3,333.67. Barrett returned there

Lawrence Barrett (1838-1891) in 1879.
COURTESY OF THE HUNTINGTON LIBRARY, SAN MARINO, CALIFORNIA

each of the next three years, and it was during a performance of *Julius Caesar* in September 1885 that an unfortunate and uncharacteristic lapse in stage management occurred. As Brutus sat musing toward the front of the stage, the curtain behind began to rise slowly, revealing the ghost of Caesar prematurely. Someone backstage could be heard shouting "No!" three different times, more frantically each time, but to no avail. "Brutus very considerately paid no attention to the spirit of Julius," a reviewer wrote, "but let him stand there and wait till the proper time should arrive for him to be greeted."[20]

America's greatest tragedian, Edwin Booth, also appeared at the Tabor Grand in April 1887, and demand for opening-night seats was so great that the management distributed tickets by auction. Receipts for Booth's initial performance as Richelieu were $3,500, far greater than usual for his first nights. He also appeared as Hamlet, Shylock, Iago in *Othello*, and Bertuccio in *The Fool's Revenge*. The *Rocky Mountain News*, often highly critical in its reviews, wrote that Booth's Hamlet was "probably the best that has ever been seen here. He is quiet and subdued... It is the Hamlet that is born of one's brain after reading and analysis, as perfect as human action can present it."[21] Booth returned to the Tabor Grand twice more, in the spring of 1888 and 1889, this time as part of the Booth and Barrett Combination, when they shared the acting honors in *Othello, Julius Caesar, Macbeth*, and other classic plays.

If Lawrence Barrett was Denver's favorite tragedian, the Polish actress Helena Modjeska might well be called Denver's most popular heroine. First appearing at the Tabor Grand on June 11, 1883, in *Camille*, she returned three times in her favorite roles of Rosalind, Camille, Juliet, Adrienne Lecouvreur, and others. During Modjeska's initial appearance, Eugene Field was up to his old tricks, reporting that someone had tried to poison her during a performance of *Romeo and Juliet* by filling Juliet's suicide phial with phosphorus. Field even printed fake interviews with most members of the cast in an attempt to uncover the conspiracy, although Modjeska herself was not available, being in bed when the reporter arrived.

In general, Denver audiences supported traditional plays (especially Shakespeare's), which made up approximately seventy-five per cent of the Tabor's repertory during its first ten years.[22] However, they also took strong exception when management used the appearance of a notable actor as an excuse to raise ticket prices. For example, when Mary Anderson came to Denver for the first and only time in March 1886,

Edwin Booth (1833–1893) as Iago in 1875.

Helena Modjeska (1840–1909) in 1884.

critics spoke out against tickets being raised to $2.00: "The truth is, New York managers are under the impression that Denver is what is termed in theatrical parlance 'a jay town' and that a good attraction is so rare as to warrant the manager who brings such to our benighted people in charging what he pleases."[23] It is certainly true that Denverites welcomed less intellectual entertainments such as comic operas, minstrel shows, magicians, and trapeze acts. Also, Denver's own critics sometimes pointed out the audience's cultural shortcomings, as when a reviewer commented on the reception of Sardou's *Daniel Rochet* in September 1882:

> [T]he piece is played without perceptibly wearing the patience of the audience. This is saying a great deal for the actors before a Western audience, as no matter how cultivated an assemblage of Western people may be, the very air that they breathe, their habits of business and customs of society incline them to the breezy side of life and they want everything to go with a vim.[24]

Yet this perception must be balanced by the impressions of the actors themselves. Lawrence Barrett was one of many performers who praised the audience's "quick, keen perception which let no point escape, however evanescent, [and] that unfailing intelligence which caught every slightest gesture and inflection."[25] When Emma Abbott called the Tabor Grand "second only to the Grand Opera House in Paris,"[26] and Edwin Booth said that he "preferred the Tabor Grand to any other theater in Europe or America,"[27] they must have been thinking partly of the knowledgeable, enthusiastic audiences as well as the magnificent theatre itself.

Wondrous and unprecedented as the Tabor Grand was, its heyday was remarkably short. With the opening of the even more splendid Broadway Theatre in 1890, the Tabor gradually yielded its reputation as Denver's leading playhouse. Those who formerly attended the opera house on Wednesday and Thursday "Society Nights" and generally cared more about seeing other playgoers than the play, began to patronize the new theatre. Meanwhile, Tabor had mortgaged the opera house in January 1891, and when he lost his fortune in the Panic of 1893 and was unable to make payments, the mortgagors tried to foreclose. After litigation lasting eighteen months, Mrs. Laura D. Smith of Denver, who held one of the two mortgages on the theatre, took possession of the Tabor Grand on September 21, 1896. Thus ended the final link of Horace Tabor with the opera house of his name, the most prized of all his possessions.

During the 1890s, the Tabor Grand continued to compete favorably with the Broadway in presenting new and classic plays, melodramas, extravaganzas, minstrel shows, and the increasingly popular light operas. Peter McCourt, manager of both the Tabor Grand and the Broadway after 1897, continued to bring first-class companies and actors to Denver through his association with the New York Syndicate of Marc Klaw and Abraham Erlanger. By the turn of the century, however, the Tabor Grand had clearly slipped in status to a second-rate but still popular theatre. As one critic remarked, "Tabor audiences like their entertainment highly seasoned. Farce comedy, gay music, and knockabout play is the thing needed. They will have that or stay at home."[28] Despite low admission prices of 75, 50, and 25 cents, the Tabor was generally more profitable than the Broadway, earning $50,000 in the 1905-6 season, $60,000 in 1906-7, with an average weekly attendance of 19,760. The Tabor also began experimenting with motion pictures in 1906, showing a film of the San Francisco earthquake and fire. But even by 1910, it was losing its audience to the more popular vaudeville and five-cent movie houses. In June 1916, McCourt bowed to the inevitable and relinquished the theatre to L. B. Vick, who operated it as a combination vaudeville and movie house.

On September 5, 1921, forty years to the day after its glittering opening night, the Tabor Grand was closed by the Denver-Colorado Theatre Company for extensive remodeling as a silent-movie palace. Little of the original theatre remained, including its name, which was changed for a time to the Colorado Theatre. In April 1929, it was renamed the Tabor Theatre and rewired for sound films. Later that same year, however, at a time when most theatrical renovations were done solely to present motion pictures, the new management enlarged the stage and improved the lighting facilities at a reported expense of $100,000, announcing, "Now, with a full stage in which to work, our patrons may expect the most colorful and talent-crammed stage presentations yet seen in the city."[29] For the next decade it often operated as a "combination theatre," presenting both first-run films and occasional live stage shows, with such stars as Judy Garland, Donald O'Connor, and the Andrews Sisters performing there. For the rest of its existence, the theatre gradually deteriorated to a second-run movie house. It was unused during parts of the 1950s and 1960s before being demolished in October 1964 with surprisingly little controversy, an inglorious end to Colorado's most fabled and fabulous theatre.

Broadway Theatre

Opened: August 18, 1890

Demolished: February 1955

The story of the Broadway Theatre begins in April 1883, when Horace Tabor brought suit against William H. Bush, his manager at the Tabor Opera House in Leadville and, in the nineteen months since its opening in 1881, the Tabor Grand in Denver. Tabor sought to recover $25,000 that he felt Bush owed him, although the grievance may have been more personal than financial: Bush allegedly did not approve of Tabor's new wife, Baby Doe, and he also hindered the advancement of her beloved brother, Peter McCourt. In winning the case with a $19,000 settlement against Bush, Tabor won the battle but lost the war. Bush, who resigned as manager of the opera house shortly after the court decision, never forgave Tabor for this insult, and as he grew wealthier through good investments and part ownership of the Windsor Hotel, he plotted to open his own theatre. When the well-known theatre manager M. B. Leavitt told Bush during a visit to Denver, "I am going to build a theatre in opposition to the Tabor Grand," Leavitt said the proposal "acted on Mr. Bush like an electric shock," and Bush immediately bundled Leavitt into a carriage to look at a promising building site that Bush owned.[30] In April 1889 Bush announced that, under a ten-year lease with Leavitt, he would build a six-story theatre, costing $250,000, on Broadway between Seventeenth and Eighteenth Avenues, to be called the Broadway Theatre.

While the Tabor Grand had been erected in the center of Denver's business district, the Broadway would compete with it from an area of the city that was less well developed but, thanks to Bush, would soon attract new business among its 133,859 residents. The theatre formed the centerpiece of the Hotel Metropole complex, flanked by the hotel entrance on one side and the hotel's restaurant on the other. (Bush already had plans at the time to construct the magnificent Brown Palace Hotel across the street from the theatre.) Built in only sixteen months after Bush's initial announcement, with Colonel J. W. Wood as architect, the building measured 80 feet wide and 175 feet in depth. The entrance to the Broadway, decorated like the rest of the hotel in red pressed brick and terra cotta, with its entrance arch trimmed in old copper, was said by one reviewer to be the most beautiful in the country.

The theatre was situated at the back of the hotel, so visitors first walked along a 130-foot hallway with a tessellated floor and marble wainscoting until they reached the theatre doors. At the entrance to the main foyer, stairways led directly to the dress circle and family circle, and one observer approved of the arrangement that "places the occupants of these tiers on terms of equality" with those fashionable patrons seated in the parquet. But it was the light and airy interior of the theatre (as opposed to the "heavy effect" of the Tabor Grand) that impressed everyone and inspired poetic rhapsodies in some, one writer calling it "a dream of beauty realized, a picture of color of rare harmonious richness, a wealth of attractiveness."[31] As one can see from the surviving photographs, Bush had clearly attempted to "out-Tabor the Tabor," and succeeded.

Exterior of the Broadway Theatre (date unknown). The arched entryway, seen between the twin towers of the Hotel Metropole complex, was decorated like the rest of the hotel in red pressed brick and terra cotta, and trimmed with old copper.
PHOTO COURTESY DENVER PUBLIC LIBRARY, WESTERN HISTORY COLLECTION, WM. HENRY JACKSON, WHJ-10365

The auditorium, beautifully decorated in shades of amber, Roman gold, and blue, was of East Indian design. Three canopy boxes flanking the stage on either side resembled Indian temples, and their gold and blue draperies were exceptionally rich in color. Thirteen smaller and less ornate foyer boxes ringed the perimeter of the parquet. The immense proscenium arch, 32 feet high and 38 and ½ feet wide, was said to be copied from one of the principal arches of the Taj Mahal, and its

Interior of the Broadway Theatre, c. 1890. Despite some obvious similarities with the Tabor Grand, the Broadway interior was thought to be light and airy compared with the "heavy effect" of its predecessor. The curtain depicted a street scene in which a procession of elephants mingled with throngs of people.

A side view of the Broadway Theatre from the stage (date unknown). The canopy boxes on the right resembled two-story Indian temples, trimmed with richly colored gold and blue draperies.
PHOTO COURTESY DENVER PUBLIC LIBRARY, WESTERN HISTORY COLLECTION X-24815

decorative trellis work, wreaths, scrolls, and tracery were based on Hindu and Saracenic architecture. This elaborate frame complemented a superb curtain, entitled "A Glimpse of India" and painted by Thomas G. Moses of Chicago, depicting a street scene in which a procession of elephants (one of them carrying a rajah waving to some Europeans, also elephant-borne) mingled with throngs of people. Despite the size of the auditorium, with a seating capacity of 1,624 (parquet 456, dress circle 502, family circle and gallery 536, boxes 130), it had a pleasing atmosphere of intimacy and warmth, with exceptionally good sightlines from every section of the theatre.

In addition to its elaborate decorations, the Broadway featured some important theatrical innovations. The stage, measuring 72 feet in width, 40 feet in depth, and 75 feet in height, was constructed of steel with a flooring of polished wood. Combined with fireproof brick and scenery coated with asbestos, the stage was "absolutely fireproof, [and] it allays the feeling of alarm and disquietude which tends so much to detract from the pleasure afforded by the entertainment to the minds of the timid."[32] A set of "Buda-Pest revolving horizons"—a clear blue sky, a sunset, and moonlight through clouds—which could serve as back-drops to all exterior scenes, was operated entirely by machinery from the stage floor. But by far the most striking feature of the Broadway was its abundant electric lighting, 1,005 incandescent bulbs in all. Nine years earlier, the Tabor had displayed a single electric light above the entrance but inside the theatre used gaslight, which at the time could be more finely modulated. A reviewer described the Broadway with these words:

> *The archway and entrance were ablaze with electric lights, and they paved the way of popularity to the hearts of the people before they reached the portals of the auditorium. In fact, the radiance of the interior of the new theater last evening can best be compared to a glimpse of fairyland. Countless incandescent lights studded a firmament of artistic frescoing over the heads of an audience of wealth, fashion, and beauty.*[33]

As this writer indicates, the combination of a lavishly ornate interior

Emma Juch (1863-1939), who opened the Broadway Theatre as Carmen in 1891.
COURTESY OF THE HUNTINGTON LIBRARY, SAN MARINO, CALIFORNIA

and brilliant lighting was suffi-cient to attract high society to the new theatre, and from opening night of August 18, 1890, the Broadway replaced the Tabor Grand as Denver's "society" the-atre. For the inaugural perform-ance, a production of *Carmen* by the Emma Juch Grand English Opera Company of New York, all tickets were sold three days before, but "The house could have been sold over again, so great was the demand."[34] Denver's leading patrons and matrons were gathered together, so that "From every box—(one might almost say from every seat)—came the scintillation of diamonds, the fra-grance of flowers, wafted along by the dainty fans of delicate lace and plumy tips."[35] Under these circumstances, it would have been almost impossible for a performance to fail, and Emma

Juch's Carmen, "most assuredly picturesque and full of a winning naivete,"[36] was received with enthusiasm. During its two-week engagement, the opera company presented eleven different operas in fourteen appearances, all sung in English, and all well attended.

With all its technical advantages and the support of Denver's social leaders, one might expect the Broadway to have seriously threatened the future of the Tabor Grand, but the story of Denver theatre in the 1890s is rather more complex. The years 1890-93, called "the Golden Age in the history of the Denver theater," brought more high-quality productions to the city than at any time before. With his well-established Silver Circuit, by which he could offer touring companies more playing dates in the Rocky Mountain region, Peter McCourt at the Tabor Grand booked such attractions as Robert Mantell, Julia Marlowe, and James O'Neill (father of the playwright Eugene O'Neill) in his famous *The Count of Monte Cristo*. The Broadway management, which contracted with the California Circuit, countered with such stars as Lotta Crabtree, "the San Francisco favorite," and Sarah Bernhardt appearing in *La Tosca, Fedora,* and *Starlight*. Bernhardt's reception in April 1891 was cooler than one might expect, with perhaps the French dialogue of her repertory being too great a hindrance to audiences.

The Silver Panic of 1893 and the resulting economic depression hit the Broadway especially hard. With the retirement of Leavitt as manager in 1893, Bush stepped in but was preoccupied with running the new Brown Palace Hotel and strapped for starring attractions. As a result, the Broadway booked only seven productions during the entire 1893-94 season and was dark from September to mid-November. Bush tried to compete with McCourt's touring shows at the Tabor Grand by presenting the H. L. Giffen and James Neill stock company during January-March 1895, with some success. He also continued to bring in touring companies, but lacking McCourt's connections with the New York Syndicate (which now virtually controlled the offerings at the Tabor Grand and on the Silver Circuit), he was restricted to those companies willing and able to play at the Broadway without other bookings in the region. In effect, McCourt's near-monopoly of theatrical talent almost put the Broadway out of business.

Events then took an unexpected turn. When Mrs. Laura D. Smith assumed ownership of the Tabor Grand in September 1896, she did not retain McCourt as manager, and he promptly joined forces with Bush at the Broadway. They brought back the Giffen-Neill Stock Company for a fifteen-week season starting in January 1897 and drew good audiences with their low ticket prices of 50 and 25 cents, compared with

$1.50 or $1.00 at the Tabor Grand. One critic charged that "the public cannot be fooled from week to week by being charged double for a play [at the Tabor Grand] when a better one can be seen at the Broadway all the season for half the price."[37] Meanwhile, when ownership of the Tabor Grand passed to the Northwestern Mutual Life Insurance Company, Bush and McCourt, through their new Colorado Amusement Company, signed a lease for the opera house on March 31, 1897, giving them control of Denver's two leading theatres. This move did not solve all their problems, for the Giffen-Neill Stock Company was losing its appeal at the Broadway, and audiences were attracted by the lower prices at Denver's other theatres, the Orpheum and Lyceum. Exasperated, Bush and McCourt sarcastically advertised, "We will bring Henry Irving and Patti, Beerbohm Tree and Nethersole, Theodore Thomas' orchestra, Duse, and the De Reszkes here and play them for 10, 20, and 30 cents, which is probably what the people want."[38]

At the start of the 1898-99 season, two events occurred that would influence the course of Denver theatre for many years: Bush died on October 12, 1898, after surgery, leaving McCourt in sole control of both the Tabor Grand and Broadway, a position he would hold for the next eighteen and thirty-one years, respectively; and the decision was made to book first-class, more expensive productions at the Broadway rather than the Tabor Grand. No reason was stated for this change in policy, but it must have involved both the upscale neighborhood of the Broadway and its superior stage and lighting facilities. The effects of this decision were seen in the repertory, with the appearance of the Lambardi Italian Opera Company at the Broadway for three weeks beginning on August 28, 1899—the longest sustained showing of grand opera in the city's history up to that time. The Metropolitan Opera Company followed the next season, and over 6,000 people saw *Tannhauser, La Boheme, Lohengrin, The Huguenots,* and *Romeo and Juliet,* with receipts for the five performances totaling $24,000. Fashionable theatregoers actually bid for seats in the boxes, with a top price of $160 for a box with eight seats. When Bernhardt and her co-star Constant-Benoît Coquelin appeared in *L'Aiglon* on February 6, 1901, the *Denver Post* wrote, "Whether people really enjoyed *L'Aiglon* or not, they were all there, and, at least, they were able to pick up valuable fashion hints from each other, for many of the gowns were the advance guard of the new spring styles."[39]

The Broadway held its status as Denver's leading theatre through the first two decades of the twentieth century, with touring companies presenting the best plays, musical comedies, and grand operas from New

York. Among the many outstanding Shakespearean actors to appear there, E. H. Sothern and Julia Marlowe in 1905, the Ben Greet Players from England in 1909, and Robert Mantell in 1908 and 1910 were especially notable. But even as early as 1901, when Helena Modjeska brought her repertory of *Henry VIII, Macbeth*, and *The Merchant of Venice* to the Broadway, lackluster audiences signaled to one critic that, "no matter how much we try to hide the apparent fact,…the classic drama is going out of fashion and the excerpts from modern life and the romantic setting of the modern spirit are coming in….We are becoming dull and heavy and demand that we be lifted from our lethargy."[40] This mood explains the growing popularity of vaudeville and the new motion pictures, both of which competed successfully for the Broadway's audiences after 1900. It also explains the popularity of *Ben Hur*, a spectacular production at the Broadway in October 1903 that featured over 200 actors, singers, and dancers, as well as twelve horses and three camels. The famous chariot race, with the horses running furiously on a treadmill while a panorama showing the arena moved in the opposite direction and electric fans blew the charioteers' garments, was exceptionally realistic and exciting.

Despite occasional headliners such as George M. Cohan's *Forty-Five Minutes from Broadway* and John Philip Sousa concerts, the critic Frank White predicted the Broadway would close for lack of attractions. "Outside managers do not want to come to Denver, for now there is nothing West for them. If the syndicate did not force them they would not come this side of the Missouri river. It is too expensive."[41] Nevertheless, the theatre had enough stars and support to stay open. It was remodeled somewhat in 1907, and the 1907-8 season proved to be the most prosperous in its history.

With the decline in quality of touring productions, which now tended to feature second-rate actors in poorly staged plays, professional theatre fell out of favor during the 1920s. Fewer companies were willing or able to afford the cross-country journey to perform in Denver, and business also suffered through competition with the movies. Still, appearances by some venerable stars in the 1930s revived the spirit of the Broadway's glory days. On July 27, 1931, Ethel Barrymore returned to perform her famous Lady Teazle in *The School for Scandal*. Although weakened by illness and castigated by one reviewer for "the most disappointing performance Miss Barrymore ever gave in Denver,"[42] she drew box-office receipts of $9,000 for four shows—the largest of her several Denver engagements over a twenty-five year period. William Gillette came out of retirement at age seventy-four to reenact the title character in his play, *Sherlock Holmes*, on January 20, 1932, "and at the final curtain fall there was an outburst of applause such as has seldom rocked the historic house."[43] Another memorable evening occurred on March 28, 1932, when Maude Adams and Otis Skinner opened in *The Merchant of Venice*. Of Maude Adams as Portia, a local critic wrote, "Her ability to dominate the stage with grandiloquent Shakespearean gestures that do not seem a bit theatrical, coupled with her vivacious spirit, enables her to carry the part. One forgets completely that Maude Adams is 60 and Skinner 74."[44]

Unfortunately, not all the stage legends appearing at the Broadway were as successful. When Walter Hampden and his company performed in *Macbeth* on April 7, 1934, the *Rocky Mountain News* responded, "With unsuspected talent, Hampden discovered humor in what everybody had believed was a blood-and-thunder tragedy, and after first conquering its amazement the audience settled down for a good laugh which burst into whoops during the closing scenes."[45]

By this date, the Broadway had begun showing motion pictures, and starting in March 1935 it regularly presented first-run films along with occasional musical productions. By 1941, few road shows appeared there. The theatre was finally torn down with little notice or protest in February 1955, another victim of the ever-growing need for parking space in downtown Denver.

Elitch's Gardens Theatre

OPENED: MAY 1, 1890

CLOSED: 1991

SCHEDULED TO REOPEN IN 2007

An early photograph of Elitch's Gardens Theatre (date unknown).
PHOTO COURTESY COLORADO HISTORICAL SOCIETY, F11956

When John Elitch, Jr., and his wife, Mary, purchased sixteen acres of farm-land a few miles outside Denver in 1887, they intended to use it mainly to supply fruits, vegetables, and dairy products for their popular Denver restaurant, the Tortoni. With its apple orchard and lovely cottonwood trees, the farm was so attractive that the Elitches were encouraged to open its grounds to the public as a park for "outing and boating parties," starting in 1889. Soon John Elitch saw the potential of his property as a full-fledged summer resort, reminiscent of the Woodward Gardens he had known in San Francisco, but a novelty in Denver. During 1889-90, he supervised the construction of a zoo, soda fountain booth, open-air café, octagonal bandstand, and, in the center of the park, a small, twelve-sided "theatorium," destined to become the longest-running summer stock theatre in the United States.

Unlike the grand opera houses built in Colorado at this time, the Elitch's Gardens Theatre was modest in size and decor. A gray wood-frame building, it contained a stage approximately 30 feet wide and 20 feet deep and accommodated an audience of approximately 600 seated on the main floor and balcony. The curtain represented the gardens themselves, Berkeley Lake, the city, and the surrounding mountains. (The famous front curtain, still extant, depicting Ann Hathaway's cottage was not added until 1894 and was always used thereafter.) For his programs, John Elitch, who had managed touring companies in the past, wanted to present vaudeville variety acts, and he hired two friends from California, Charles W. Goodyear and Charles E. Schilling, to help manage the theatre and engage several vaudevillians for the premiere. Admission price to the park was 25 cents for adults and 10 cents for children, which included access to both the gardens and theatre.

The grand opening of the park, scheduled for 11:00 a.m. on May 1, 1890, did not appear promising because of a morning rainfall. However, shortly before that hour, a friend galloped up on horseback and shouted to Elitch, "John! Get ready to open! The whole town's on its way here." With the Berkeley Motor, a trolley car, as the only public transportation from the center of Denver to Elitch's park on the north side (located at the corner of Tennyson and West 38th Streets), the transfer station in north Denver was jammed with would-be travelers for several blocks. When the train arrived, Mrs. Elitch recalled:

> *Men forgot their wives in the attempt to get aboard. . . . Some people lost portions of their attire, and one man actually had his trousers torn off. . . . The roof of every car was covered with people; others clung to the sides, and even the front of the engine held men. . . . Other thousands walked through the mud all the way from the city and back again.*[46]

Once they arrived at the park, "Pandemonium broke loose. Men shouted and danced, and tossed their hats into the air. Women laughed and cheered and hugged their friends. Even the most dignified men and women surrendered to the holiday spirit."[47] These dignitaries included Horace Tabor, Governor John L. Routt, and Denver mayor Wolfe Londoner, as well as theatre celebrities Julia Marlowe, P. T. Barnum, and Nat Goodwin, all friends of Elitch's from his early days in the San Francisco theatre.

After a picnic accompanied by a band performance, the crowd packed into the theatre and under the surrounding trees (since the sides were not enclosed until the following season) to hear some brief, complimentary remarks by the mayor, followed by the raising of the curtain for the first time. Typical of vaudeville at the time, the opening program featured, among other acts, the Montgomerys ("Comedy Sketch—Banjoists), Miss Minnie Zola ("The Little Athletic Wonder"), Van Auken and La Van ("Champion Triple Horizontal Bar Performers of the World"), co-manager Charles E. Schilling ("The Quaint, Comical Musical Genius"), and the Emily Zola Troupe from Australia ("Most

John Elitch, Jr. (1850–1891).
PHOTO COURTESY DENVER PUBLIC
LIBRARY, WESTERN HISTORY
COLLECTION, F-2460

Expert and Daring Artists That Have Ever Visited This Country"). A reviewer noted approvingly, "There was nothing heavy about the show. There was nothing unseemly. It was clean and bright throughout. Any man could have taken his wife and little ones to see it, and all would have enjoyed it."[48]

Mary Elitch (1850–1936).
PHOTO COURTESY COLORADO HISTORICAL
SOCIETY, F38619

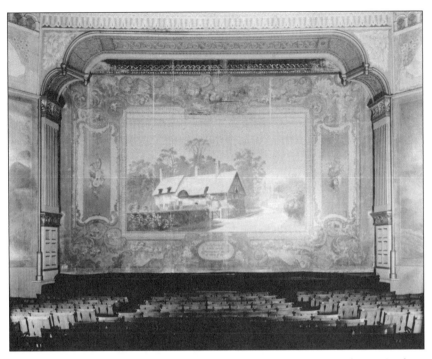

The well-known drop curtain of Elitch's Gardens Theatre (date unknown). The curtain showed (as the inscription at the bottom states) "Anne Hathaway's cottage a mile away/Shakespeare sought at close of day."
PHOTO COURTESY DENVER PUBLIC LIBRARY, WESTERN HISTORY COLLECTION, X-24648

This first season of vaudeville lasted till October 19, and a typical seven-act program featured such audience favorites as acrobats, jugglers, female impersonators, and animal acts. With a profit of $35,000, Elitch revived his old dream and, together with Goodyear and Schilling, organized a new minstrel company to travel the Silver Circuit, then along the Pacific Coast. When the troupe reached San Francisco, Elitch suddenly became ill and died of pneumonia on March 10, 1891.

The owner's untimely death led to the purchase of Elitch's Gardens in May 1891 by a corporation of nine Denver businessmen. The theatre programs went on much as before, with vaudeville and light opera sharing most of the programs, and the addition of gas lighting in 1891 permitted evening as well as matinee performances. In 1893 the Frank Norcross Company presented the first season of summer stock in Denver's history, beginning on June 10 with *Nancy and Company.* However, not even Elitch's Gardens's considerable success could withstand the Panic of 1893, and it was placed in receivership, which gave

A matinee crowd gathers outside Elitch's Gardens Theatre between 1900 and 1910.
PHOTO COURTESY DENVER PUBLIC LIBRARY, WESTERN HISTORY COLLECTION, L. C. McCLURE, MCC-1226

Mary Elitch, the "Lady of the Gardens," the opportunity to regain ownership in March 1894 for a price of $150,000.

Thus began what might be called Elitch's Golden Age, the period from 1894 to 1915, when the resident stock company gradually replaced vaudeville as the theatre's main attraction during a season lasting from the second week of June till Labor Day week. There were several reasons for the theatre's popularity during this time. First, the stock companies of ten to sixteen actors were consistently high in quality, the company members being selected by auditions in New York. They in turn were attracted to Elitch's by the prospect of summer work, the growing reputation of the theatre, and Denver's pleasant summer climate. Second, Mary Elitch, who became the theatre's manager in 1897, kept ticket prices low, ranging from 50 to 10 cents. She was also extremely conscientious in delivering the advertised programs and not canceling a performance. In August 1908, when a thunderstorm disabled the tramways and delayed the start of David Warfield's popular starring vehicle, *The Music Master*, "there were no murmurs from those who had to get there on time, and had to wait, nor any diminution in the enthusiasm when the curtain finally went up at 9:30 p.m."[49] Third, the theatre itself continued to be remodeled so it was more commodious and comfortable, although through the years it retained its basic shape and became a well-known landmark. In 1896, for example, the theatre was repainted, the stage was enlarged (to 90 feet wide and 40 feet deep), and ten new boxes were added. By 1904, it could seat 1,419 people, and in 1907 twelve pagoda boxes (apparently inspired by those at the Tabor Grand and Broadway) were added near the stage; eight of those boxes remain today.

At a time when Elitch's was the only non-Syndicate theatre in Denver, Mary Elitch used her theatre connections to bring in such independent stars as Sarah Bernhardt, Minnie Maddern Fiske, and David Warfield, "instead of relying supinely upon the careless generosity of the syndicate."[50] In addition, Douglas Fairbanks made his stage debut at Elitch's in 1895 when he was twelve years old, James O'Neill (honoring a promise he had made to John Elitch when the theatre was being constructed) performed in *Helene* in the summer of 1897, and Cecil B. DeMille acted minor roles there in the summer of 1905. He later referred to Elitch's as "what all actors and actresses consider one of the greatest cradles of the drama in American history." In response to competition from a rival summer theatre at Manhattan Beach (opened in 1891), Elitch's offered not only its standard fare of comedy, light opera, vaudeville, and farce, but special attractions such as The Brothers Leondor, "in classical gladiatorial groupings;" Dyrene, a "transformation dancer;" T. F. Grant, the one-legged song and dance expert; and most notably, the Edison Vitascope, shown in 1896 for the first time in Denver, featuring "the Leigh sisters in their umbrella dance…[and] the breaking of waves on the sea shore:"

> [T]he effect was simply marvelous, wave after wave came tumbling on the sand and as they struck and broke into tiny floods just like the real thing, some of the people in the front row seemed to think they were going to get wet and looked about to see where they could run to in case the waves came too close.[51]

Mrs. Elitch finally eliminated the rivalry problem by purchasing Manhattan Beach in January 1900.

On July 17, 1900, Elitch's celebrated its fifteen-hundredth performance with a production of *The Dancing Girl* that starred Blanche Bates and drew standing-room audiences. On this occasion, *Denver Post* reviewer Frank White, who had often criticized the quality of Elitch's acting companies, wrote, "It is simply marvelous to reflect that from the small beginnings of a dozen years ago the Gardens, world-wide famed, have arisen to their present splendid position of maintaining the most expensive and perfect stock company in the United States. The growth of Elitch's is a matter of civic pride and civic history."[52] The following summer, when Mary Elitch-Long (having married T. D. Long in November 1900) instituted the "visiting star" system, profits for the season were estimated at $10,000.

As one would expect in a summer theatre, the repertory was mostly "light" and undemanding, but during 1899-1908, director

Walter Clarke Bellows presented a more ambitious selection of plays. In 1899 he staged the first production of *Cyrano de Bergerac* ever seen in Denver, with a seventy-four member cast. He also directed nine productions of Shakespeare's plays over a ten-year period. The difficulties of handling Shakespeare's blank verse, large casts, and scenic requirements were formidable, and the strain sometimes showed. Yet with *As You Like It*, in a creative piece of staging, the back wall of the theatre was removed so that the backdrop for the play became the surrounding trees and meadows.

Elitch's persevered successfully during these years not only with Shakespeare, but with modern works such as Ibsen's *A Doll's House* and *Rosmersholm* (the latter starring Minnie Maddern Fiske in June 1908), Shaw's *Man and Superman* and *You Never Can Tell*, and realistic plays such as *The City* and *Salvation Nell*. Critic Frank White was so repulsed by the barroom scenes in *Salvation Nell* that he called it "the apotheosis of the brutish" and "one of the most degraded entertainments ever given in Denver.... I would certainly no more permit my daughter, or young son, to visit the drama at the Gardens this week than I would take them on a pleasure tour through the dens of Market Street, or introduce them to the degraded inmates of the county jail."[53]

There were other hazards sometimes associated with Elitch's. In September 1905, a *Denver Times* reviewer criticized the acting and dancing of Maude Fealy, a perennial Denver favorite, only to have her stepfather storm the newspaper office in her defense:

> *With fire in his eyes and abuse on his tongue, Signor Faffaelo Cavallo, a most excellent musician and the most loyal husband of Miss Fealy's mother, hurried to the Times office early Monday morning and within three minutes had precipitated a 'rough house.' The excited stepfather of Miss Fealy was led downstairs by an acquaintance, who advised him to put himself in cold storage for a few hours and think the matter over.*[54]

The occasional shocking play or offstage incident had little to do with the decline in Elitch's audiences that began in 1912. Rather, competition from local theatres, rising production costs, the popularity of movies, the increased use of automobiles for day trips and vacations, even unusually cold and rainy weather—all combined to erode the theatre's profits until it was forced to close in mid-season on August 14, 1915. It was sold the following year to a local businessman, John M. Mulvihill, for $35,000, but it remained mostly closed over the next four seasons.

Fortunately, Mulvihill was determined to maintain the Elitch's traditions, and the productions at the theatre during 1920-31 were both artistic and popular. Mulvihill was helped by the decline in the number of road companies touring the country. During this period, resident stock companies like Elitch's were often the only means for audiences to see the latest Broadway hits, and the companies therefore had access to a wider repertory than before. Like Mary Elitch, he hired seasoned directors such as Melville Burke and talented actors who were eager to advance their careers by performing at Elitch's. For example, Frederic March was still relatively unknown when he was chosen as the company's leading man for three seasons, 1926-28. He performed in thirty-four plays, becoming one of Elitch's most popular actors. He later recalled: "The experience was wonderful; I had the opportunity to play tremendously exciting roles I never would have been able to do in New York.... I relished the chance to experiment and to enlarge characterizations."[55] March, like many other actors, was attracted by "the tradition of the place. At that time it was known all over the East and it was considered a feather in the cap of an actor to have played a season at Elitch's. Anyone who was successful there had an excellent chance of getting better parts when he returned to New York."[56] Some consequences could be serious, however. In 1926, March broke Mulvihill's rule that the leading man and lady could not be married, the manager believing that no one would pay to see a man court his wife on stage. When March married actress Florence Eldridge anyway, Mulvihill dismissed her from the company.

Frederic March (1897-1975), leading man at Elitch's from 1926-1928 (date unknown).
PHOTO COURTESY HISTORIC ELITCH THEATRE FOUNDATION

By the time of Mulvihill's management, audiences had established what was called "The Elitch Habit," meaning that certain types of playgoers attended the theatre on particular days. The most avid theatregoers and the newspaper critics wanted to be there for openings on Sunday nights. Monday continued to be "society night," when Denver's prominent citizens wished to be seen, then read about themselves in the next day's paper. Wednesday and Saturday matinees were frequented by large numbers of women, and Friday and Saturday evenings were family nights. Whatever the day, Elitch's audiences were attentive and receptive. Frederic March said, "I'll always remember the warmth of the audiences. Footlights were no barrier to them; you could sense audience responses there more acutely than any other theatre I know."[57]

When Mulvihill died in 1930, the theatre was handed down to his son-in-law, Arnold B. Gurtler. Like Mulvihill, he was something of a theatrical novice who left the productions in the hands of experienced directors like George Somnes, who produced sixty-five plays at Elitch's from 1936 to 1947. Gurtler was also a preserver of tradition. "Like the 'Church Around the Corner' and Henry Ford's 'Little Red Schoolhouse,'" he wrote, "there is another building in America which has not been affected by modernism. Elitch's frame theatre building has remained unchanged through the years.... Anyone who has beheld the charm of this historic old playhouse at the end of a winding path through the apple orchard would readily appreciate the sentiment attached to it."[58] On June 16, 1941, Elitch's marked the opening of its fiftieth season with a gala Golden Anniversary celebration, with Don Woods and Ruth Matteson starring together in a number of plays that season, directed by George Somnes.

Through the years, Elitch's continued to attract up-and-coming stars, although Gurtler's judgment was not infallible. During one of his casting trips to New York, he met a young actor who was too inexperienced to qualify for Elitch's. Gurtler wrote in his casting notes, "I saw Clark Gable today. A very fine young man, but he ought to get his ears fixed."[59] A happier outcome occurred in the summer of 1951 when, a few days after a young actress had arrived for the season, a woman came to the theatre and announced to Gurtler, "I'm Mrs. Kelly from Philadelphia and I want to see my daughter." As Gurtler's son Jack explained, "Mrs. Kelly probably figured her daughter was way out here in the west in some broken-down summer stock company and would end up stranded before the season was over."[60] Instead, Grace Kelly, age 21, acted in every play that season, and her mother was so charmed by Elitch's Gardens that she decided to spend the summer with her. Under the "star system," which replaced the old summer stock company beginning in 1964, such well-known actors as Walter Pidgeon, Debbie Reynolds, Shelly Winters, James Whitmore, Ginger Rogers, Kim Hunter, and Lynn Redgrave also appeared on Elitch's venerable stage.

Eventually, though, the time came when actors who had once jumped at the chance to perform at Elitch's were increasingly drawn to the greater rewards and publicity of movies and television. It became more difficult to draw large houses with touring productions, even with seventy to eighty per cent of ticket sales going to season-ticket holders, and 1988 marked the last full summer season of theatre. In 1991, a production of *The Robber Bridegroom* was the last to appear at Elitch's, and after 101 years of continuous summer stock, the theatre closed and remains dark.

A preservation effort led by Denver Mayor Wellington Webb and City Councilman Dennis Gallagher resulted in the theatre being named a Designated Denver Landmark and forestalled a proposal to move it to another location in Denver. The Board and staff of the Historic Elitch Gardens Theatre Foundation are working with the property owners to preserve the building and continue the theatre's life as a non-profit cultural center for theatre, dance, music, and film. The Foundation intends to restore the original appearance of the theatre down to the paint colors, pagoda boxes, and 1894 curtain. Unlike its regal counterparts, the Tabor Grand and the Broadway, this Denver landmark is poised to begin its second century of entertainment for Denver audiences.

CHAPTER FOUR

LEADVILLE AND ASPEN

LEADVILLE

Tabor Opera House

OPENED: NOVEMBER 20, 1879

CURRENTLY UNDERGOING REHABILITATION

Leadville in 1879 was a wide-open boomtown full of gambling houses, dance halls, and saloons. Miners had been in the area for almost twenty years looking for gold, but in 1876 silver-rich deposits of lead carbonate were found and Leadville, the two-mile-high city, was born two years later. By 1879 the population stood at 5,040. A year later it tripled to almost 15,000.

It was appropriate that the first mayor of Leadville, the richest of silver camps, should be its richest man, Horace Tabor. Born in Vermont in 1830, Tabor homesteaded in Kansas before being drawn to Colorado by reports of gold strikes in 1859. With his industrious, frugal wife, Augusta, he set up a series of general stores in mountain mining camps, including Oro City and Buckskin Joe, while prospecting, serving as postmaster, and grubstaking hundreds of new miners.

For almost twenty years the Tabors scraped along, never wealthy, but better off than most of the hard-luck miners around them. In 1877 they moved to what would become Leadville, and Tabor's years of grub-staking finally paid off: two unpromising-looking miners, George Hook and August Rische, struck a rich vein of silver carbonate at the Little Pittsburg Mine. Tabor received thirty per cent of a mine that at its height produced $10,000 of silver ore a day.[1]

Tabor used his money to buy more mines, invest in banks, and otherwise build a substantial fortune. With money came position, and by 1879 he was Colorado's lieutenant governor, a largely ceremonial position he held while retaining the mayoralty of Leadville. He also become president of two phone companies and served as an officer in prosperous banks. Although his time and attention were increasingly diverted from Leadville, he had high aspirations for the town. His public generosity was remarkable: he constructed a gas plant, and also organized and outfitted both a fire brigade and a local military company.

Tabor recognized that there was a need for legitimate theatre in his up-and-coming town. While banks, hotels, and other signs of city respectability were going up, entertainment for the locals primarily took place at its numerous watering holes. Variously called saloons, saloon-theatres, and variety theatres, most featured entertaining barmaids, piano players, and liberal quantities of drink. They were everywhere: in 1879, Leadville had four banks, five churches, about twenty hotels—and eighty-two saloons. Pap Wyman's Saloon, also called Pap Wyman's Concert and Dance Hall, was a typical institution in the 1880s. Offering every kind of gambling and cards, it had a variety theatre as well as scantily clad barmaids, dancing, and drinking. Pap was a man of scruples, however. House rules

Horace Austin Warner Tabor (1830-1899), Colorado's "Silver King," built opera houses in both Leadville and Denver before losing his fortune in the early 1890s (date unknown).
PHOTO COURTESY DENVER PUBLIC LIBRARY, WESTERN HISTORY COLLECTION, Z-229

declared that drunken men would not be served at the bar and that no married man was allowed at the gambling tables. Over the face of a large wall clock was painted the gentle remonstrance, "Please Don't Swear." And Pap also posted the famous admonition, "Don't shoot the Pianist. He's doing his Damndest."[2]

Admonitions or no, Pap's was no place for a family in search of uplifting entertainment. Horace Tabor responded to this need by announcing he would donate the land and money to build an opera house, an initiative Tabor's biographer, Duane Smith, calls "the capstone of his [Leadville] projects."[3] Tabor determined to spare no expense on his theatre, which he situated on Harrison Avenue next to the town's finest hotel, the Clarendon.

He originally hired L. E. and J. Thomas Roberts to build his opera house for a sum of $30,000. (Final cost estimates were considerably higher, ranging from $40,000 to $78,000.) Most materials were not available in Leadville and had to be hauled by wagon over Weston Pass from the closest railroad connection at Webster. Still, the construction went along at a furious pace, as recounted in the *Leadville Daily Chronicle* just before the opening on November 20, 1879:

> *That large fine-fronted massively-built brick building on Harrison Avenue fifteen feet beyond the Clarendon Hotel is Tabor's Opera house. Ground was broke for its foundation just one hundred days ago tomorrow morning. . . . [N]owhere in the West has that amount of money created so creditable a building.*[4]

Early exterior of the Tabor Opera House, Leadville (date unknown). The third-story catwalk on the right connected the opera house to the Clarendon Hotel for the convenience of hotel guests and actors.

Entrance to the three-story building was through a vestibule, which in turn opened onto an imposing lobby surmounted by a wide, carpeted staircase that conveyed patrons into the theatre, located on the second floor. The sparkling auditorium measured 57 feet wide by 65 feet deep and had a color scheme of white, gold, red, and sky blue. There was par-quet-level seating for 450 and a horseshoe gallery that could seat 400 more. Tabor had Andrews patent orchestra seats installed on the main floor, identical to those in the finest theatres in New York. They were made of filigreed gilt cast iron, comfortably upholstered in red velvet and had wire hat racks mounted below the seats. Plain wooden benches filled the gallery. The Tabor also had the distinction of being the first gas-lit building in town, Tabor's gas works having been completed to coincide with the theatre's opening. The *Daily Chronicle* reviewer continued:

> *The aisles are beautifully carpeted; and the ceilings to the hall are handsomely frescoed; the ventilation is perfect; the blending beauty of the whole being fully brought out by brightly burning lights from sev-enty-two jets. The entire house is furnace warmed; the fire extinguish-ing arrangements are perfect; in fact to tell the whole story in one chapter, Tabor's Opera House in Leadville is the most perfect place of amusement between Chicago or St. Louis and San Francisco.*[5]

Mirrored and velvet-draped proscenium boxes, in two tiers, flanked the stage. They contained hand-carved, richly upholstered chairs and handsome carpets; the drapery was trimmed with fine lace. A uni-formed fifteen-piece orchestra could be seated in a semicircle before the stage at parquet level.

The stage itself, called "one of the largest west of New York,"[6] measured 58 feet wide by 35 feet deep; the backstage area was 34 feet high, allowing for storage of the extensive scenery above the stage. The hand-painted stage curtain depicted, appropriately enough, a stream running through a mountain landscape, although the castle perched alongside it was somewhat incongruous. Above the curtain hung a life-size portrait of Tabor.

While four sets of scenery were considered standard for a theatre, the Tabor had at least seven, including a prison scene and a New England-style kitchen.[7] All were painted by J. B. Lamphere, a respected scene painter in the West. Perhaps the most interesting drop was a vision of Leadville's main street on the Fourth of July 1881, with a series of shad-owy buildings fading into the distant sky, suggesting the town's future sky-line. Most of the scenery is still in existence, stored at the theatre.[8]

Despite the handsome surroundings, the first-night audience on November 20, 1879, was unexpectedly somber, due to the lynching of two men the night before just down the street from the opera house. The reviewer for the *Leadville Herald Democrat* explained, "Theatre goers were in no mood for frivolity, accounting for poor atten-dance."[9] However, on subse-quent nights the stock company engaged for thirteen weeks by Tabor played to mostly full houses. Since there was still no rail link to Leadville, Tabor wisely con-tracted with Jack Langrishe, the popular mining camp enter-tainer, to perform with his troupe for the entire season. The opening-night offering, a French adaptation called *The Serious Family,* was coupled with a curtain raiser written by Langrishe himself, entitled *Who's Who.* The *Leadville Weekly Herald* reported in its

Engraving of the stage, boxes, and orchestra pit of the Tabor Opera House, Leadville, as they appeared shortly after its opening in November 1879.
PHOTO COURTESY DENVER PUBLIC LIBRARY, WESTERN HISTORY COLLECTION, C917.8846 L469

December 6, 1879 issue that "The Tabor opera house has attracted many of the pleasure seekers of the city, for every night a new piece has been produced, and Jolly Jack and his admirable company have made enviable names for themselves as the pioneers of the legitimate drama in Leadville."[10] Three or four plays were performed each week, except Sundays, when the theatre was closed. Reserved seats in the parquet sold for $1.50, and gallery seats cost 50 cents. The popular Irish playwright Dion Boucicault had five of his plays performed, along with others by Shakespeare, Augustin Daly, Edward Bulwer-Lytton, and Lester Wallack.

The first touring group to appear at the Tabor was Jack Haverly's Church Choir, later called Haverly's Mastodon Minstrels. Booked initially in April 1880, when they performed *H.M.S. Pinafore*, Haverly's was among the best known of the nation's many touring blackface groups, and the company made many subsequent appearances in Leadville.

Two of the most enthusiastically received productions of that first season were for the same play, d'Ennery's melodrama *The Two Orphans*. Kate Claxton, whose name was so firmly associated with the play that she eventually bought the performance rights and toured it exclusively for many years, appeared first in April 1881. Shortly thereafter, the Langrishe company, still in residence, mounted its own production. Leadville theatregoers, "prepared for faultfinding and adverse criticism," nonetheless loyally supported the interpretation of the Langrishe company's leading lady, Miss Phosa McAllister, in the role of blind Louise. The *Daily Chronicle* reviewer claimed the audience was "[t]he largest and most fashionable . . . that ever congregated within amusement walls in this city. . . . Last night it was not looked for—so strong an exhibition of dramatic powers—and took the house by storm. Too much cannot be said in praise of the Louise of Miss McAllister."[11]

Tabor's opera house lent a much-needed air of gentility to hard-living Leadville, but reality wasn't far away: just behind the druggist's shop that occupied one of the storefronts on the first floor of the opera house was a saloon, serving thirsty playgoers between acts. The store-front on the other side of the opera house entrance was let to a men's clothier, Sands, Pelton & Co. Its owner, Jake Sands, was a friend of a beautiful young divorcée from Central City, Elizabeth McCourt Doe. Better known as Baby Doe, she followed Sands to Leadville and eventually met and was courted there by the man who would become her second husband, Horace Tabor.

The opera house also included a sumptuous suite of living quarters and offices for Augusta and Horace Tabor, and Tabor's business partner, William Bush. Located on the second floor, with large windows facing Colorado's highest peaks, Mount Elbert and Mount Massive, these elegantly appointed rooms served as the Tabors' home whenever they were in Leadville. Completing the building's space on the third floor were additional offices, a storeroom, and a number of small rooms to put up actors and serve as overflow for the Clarendon Hotel next door.

As the town's new civic center, the Tabor was thrust into a different kind of prominence when a miner's strike was declared in May 1880, triggered by dissatisfaction with low wages and fear of declining output. The opera house became the headquarters for mine owners and even housed the National Guard when panicky owners felt the local militia was outmanned. Fortunately, threats to set fire to the Tabor never materialized. The miners' demands went unmet and the situation returned to normal after only a few days, including the briefly interrupted schedule of entertainment at the opera house.[12]

On a happier note, 1880 also brought the railroad to Leadville. The narrow-gauge Denver & Rio Grande, owned by William Jackson Palmer, beat out competition from the Atchison, Topeka & Santa Fe and arrived in Leadville on July 22. The race had not been easy. A battle over right of way through the Royal Gorge wound up before the Supreme Court, which ruled in favor of Palmer's "Baby Road."

The opera house figured prominently in the celebration over the railroad's arrival. Former President and Mrs. Ulysses S. Grant were passengers on the first train and were lavishly entertained for five days. After greeting the several bands, choirs, and throngs of Leadville residents from a platform outside the opera house, President Grant and his retinue retired to the Tabor box inside to see a production of *Our Boarding House*, performed by a descendant of Langrishe's company known as the Knowles

Troupe. Before they left, the same group performed T. W. Robertson's *Ours*, a popular British comedy.[13]

The arrival of the railroad made it possible for the best of Broadway to come to Leadville. Touring companies previously reached the town by stagecoach, as when the original New York cast of *The Banker's Daughter* appeared in June 1880. Written by the social reformer Bronson Howard, the play was enthusiastically received.[14] Nevertheless, stage travel was difficult through the rugged mountains and narrow passes. Evelyn Furman, present owner of the

Otis Skinner (1858–1942) in an unidentified role (date unknown).

Tabor Opera House, quotes an anonymous letter that tells of a stage rolling over six times on its trip to Leadville.[15]

Even with enthusiastic audiences and improved accessibility, Leadville, the highest incorporated town in the United States, was a taxing place to perform due to its extreme altitude. Otis Skinner, a leading Shakespearean actor of his day, recalled in his memoirs his 1883 appearance as Marc Antony in *Julius Caesar* as "nearly disastrous. . . . By the time I had reached the middle of the big speech, I was all in. The blood was pounding in my ears and in my temples, and my chest was heaving in asthmatic convulsions. . . . [W]hen the calls came I had only strength enough to fall out in front of the curtain and to fall back again."[16]

Oscar Wilde, British aesthete and playwright, appeared at the Tabor in 1882. Rowdy Leadville miners took an unexpected liking to the affected Wilde, who reciprocated, calling his stop in Leadville the highlight of his American tour.
PHOTO COURTESY DENVER PUBLIC LIBRARY, WESTERN HISTORY COLLECTION, HARPERS WKLY, JAN. 7TH, 1882, F-23042

Perhaps the most memorable of all those who appeared on Leadville's opera house stage in the early days was the Irish poet, playwright, and aesthete Oscar Wilde, who later pronounced his stay there as the highlight of his American tour. He arrived in October 1882 dressed like a miner and immediately was faint from the altitude. Pronounced fit, he appeared that evening on the stage in a cutaway jacket, velvet knee breeches, ruffled shirt, and very long hair.[17] Singular as his appearance must have been to Leadvillites, his lecture topic on aesthetic theory was even more curious. In the midst of silver miners, he expounded upon Benvenuto Cellini, the sixteenth-century Italian silversmith. Asked why he had not brought Mr. Cellini along, Wilde explained that he was long dead, to which an audience member queried, "Who shot him?"[18]

It was only after the lecture, on a tour of the town with Tabor and other locals, that the skepticism of the miners turned to appreciation. The convivial banquet held in Wilde's honor at the bottom of the Matchless Mine convinced everyone of Wilde's worth, since he held his liquor so well. Wilde later commented, "The amazement of the miners when they saw that art and appetite could go hand in hand knew no bounds…. The first course was whiskey, the second whiskey, the third whiskey, all the courses were whiskey, but still they called it supper."[19] In honor of his visit, a new mining shaft was opened, named "The Oscar." To Wilde's disappointment, he was not offered shares in its development.

Nevertheless, he came to like the miners and later, when asked about their coarseness, declared them "Ready, but not rough. They were polished and refined compared with the people I met in larger cities farther East."[20]

Wilde's stay in Leadville was memorable, but he was by no means the only headline-making visitor. Crowds thronged to see Fannie Louise Buckingham and her company perform the titillating drama, *Mazeppa*, in which the hero (often played by a woman, as in this instance) in the last act is lashed in somewhat revealing attire to the back of a charging horse. The reviewer was much impressed by both Miss Buckingham and her horse, Melville, which he

Fannie Louise Buckingham as Mazeppa
(date unknown).

proclaimed "a noble specimen … full of life and vim." The equestrian display was spectacular, prompting the reviewer to note, "It almost makes one shudder to see it, and we think that the audience fully appreciate that one misstep would be almost instant death for the fair rider."[21]

Little did audience members realize that the real drama was being played out in rehearsal. In a front-page article entitled "On Her High Horse," the *Leadville Daily Herald* reported that Miss Buckingham, suspecting her husband of a liaison with another member of the company, "swooped down upon her alleged faithless husband . . . [on] her fiery steed, flew up the run way and then threatened to ride down every one upon the stage, including the astonished stage hands, who stood about in open mouthed wonder. . . . [S]he determined to prove to the trembling husband . . . that there can be a hell on earth."[22]

It is often said that the Tabor Opera House never had an opera performed on its stage. The reverse is true: Leadville was treated to a remarkable number of operatic productions, especially considering its size and isolation. The Emma Abbott English Opera Company tour of September 1882 is a good example. Appearing to overflowing houses in the then-popular operas *The Chimes of Normandy* and *King for a Day,* the ensemble was led by Emma Abbott herself in the leading roles. The reviewer was rhapsodic in his praise and reported that Miss Abbott "gained the laurel crown of the evening and roused the large audience to a pitch of enthusiasm that, for a moment, hardly knew bounds."[23] The appreciation was reciprocated when Miss Abbott tried her hand at panning for gold during her stay in Leadville. Her first, painstaking effort yielded about fifteen cents in gold. "Oh, dear me," Miss Abbott exclaimed, "and I thought it was rather easy to mine. I guess I'd rather sing after all."[24] Most years, multiple opera companies were booked into Leadville, performing everything from light to grand opera.

The early 1880s were the glory days of the Tabor Opera House, but by 1883 the beginning of a long decline had set in for Leadville, its opera house, and Horace Tabor. Augusta had left the town in 1880; she divorced Horace in 1883, making way for his notorious marriage to Baby Doe in Washington, D.C., later that year. Mines played out and performers steadily shortened their stays as the population dwindled, until by the end of the decade, Leadville was only a one-night stand on the Silver Circuit.

Still, there were glorious performances, even if they occurred less frequently than before. James H. Cragg arrived in March 1882 to become the manager of the opera house, a position he held for more than a decade, in addition to being manager of the telephone exchange and a nearby Turkish bath. He arranged for the great Shakespearean actor Lawrence Barrett to appear in warmly received productions of *Francesca da Rimini* and *Julius Caesar* in June 1883.[25] Less enthusiasm was shown to social reformer Henry Ward Beecher when he arrived to lecture on luxury, beauty, and morality the same year. Beecher's support of the theory of evolution and women's suffrage probably did not endear him to his conservative Leadville audience.[26]

Renowned Polish actress Helena Modjeska first appeared in Leadville in 1884, acting in two of her most popular roles as Rosalind in *As You Like It* and as Viola in *Twelfth Night.* She returned two years later to perform more Shakespeare as well as a number of other roles. Lotta Crabtree, "the San Francisco favorite," and Emma Abbott's opera company also booked return engagements in the latter half of the decade, adding light to an otherwise fading list of attractions. Newspapers from these years have largely vanished, leaving us only to speculate on these actresses' receptions in the self-proclaimed "Cloud City."

The entertainment calendar from the *Herald Democrat* for 1886 gives a good sense of the types of attractions booked into the opera house and their popularity. The best-attended event of the year was McNish, Slavin, and Johnson's minstrels, who appeared four times before a combined audience of 2,340. Close behind them was the series of performances of *The Mikado, The Sorcerer,* and *Fatinitza* given by the Chicago Opera. Large audiences also came to see James O'Neill in *The Count of Monte Cristo* and George S. Knight's two performances in *Over the Garden Wall.* Other entertainments for the year ranged from large to small: the Milan Opera Company produced *Il Trovatore, Faust,* and *Lucia di Lammermoor;* a booking for J. H. Brown, mind reader, followed immediately. *Uncle Tom's Cabin* reappeared, as did Helena Modjeska, both drawing an equal number of attendees. Sometimes performers stopped for three evenings and a matinee, but one- and two-night engagements were more common.[27]

Ironically, the improvement of rail access to Leadville at the beginning of the 1890s hastened the establishment of the town as a one-night stand. Since it was easier for companies to get to Leadville, more booked it, but it was correspondingly easier to leave as well, so that Silver Circuit entertainers saw no reason to linger. In 1890 the Tabor hosted more than one hundred engagements, including such notables as Shakespearean actor Robert Mantell and popular actress Effie Ellsler, in one of her nine appearances on the Tabor stage. Light opera, vaudeville, and minstrel shows also appeared, along with a number of home talent shows. Still trying to promote the town's uniqueness, the New Year's edition of the *Herald Democrat* for 1891 rather plaintively boasted the superiority of its climate for local theatres: "The weather is so delightfully cool throughout the summer months at this altitude, that no discomfort is experienced in sitting

A home talent production from the Tabor Opera House's first decade.
PHOTO COURTESY DENVER PUBLIC LIBRARY, WESTERN HISTORY COLLECTION, X-181

through a three hours' attraction, and fans and ice water are almost unknown in our places of amusement."[28]

The declining fortunes of the town were summed up when, in March 1893, Horace Tabor was forced to sell the opera house. Badly overextended, Tabor had sold or mortgaged everything he owned in the early 1890s. The Leadville opera house was one of his last properties. Fittingly, he sold it to another longtime Leadville resident, Judge A. S. Weston, a miner and attorney who had lived in Leadville almost as long as Tabor. Judge Weston bought the Tabor for $22,000 and changed little but its name. "The Weston" continued to serve as the cultural center of Leadville until the judge's death four years later, when his wife took over the theatre's management.[29]

Although Mrs. L. B. Weston, one of a handful of women theatre owners of her time, struggled to bring in first-rate entertainment, more often than not vaudeville and minstrel shows filled the bill. Early motion picture prototypes such as the "Wonderful Magniscope" also were shown.[30] Interestingly, the *Herald Democrat*, in its evaluation of the amusements of 1898, describes the opera house, built only twenty years before, as "[t]he old Tabor Grand theater, erected in the palmy days of the camp," but declares it "is still Leadville's leading amusement resort."[31] Open ten to fifteen nights a month, the opera house boasted few top-flight companies, with no Shakespeare or grand opera among the year's engagements. In September 1899, however, a remarkable highlight occurred when the Metropolitan Opera Company booked the opera house for a week to perform eight different operas. Daily exhortations appeared in the *Herald Democrat* encouraging townspeople to attend and reminding them of the exceptional quality and value the opportunity presented. Ticket prices were extremely low: four dollars purchased reserved seats to all eight performances.[32] Although reviews were perfunctory, attendance was good, and these performances were considered the best of the decade.

Only eight years after Tabor lost the opera house, its ownership changed twice within a matter of weeks: Dr. J. H. Heron bought the theatre in July 1901 for $12,000, only to sell it to the Leadville Chapter of Elks in September. The Elks operated the theatre for less than a year before closing it for a thorough remodeling, although during that time they brought in the Chicago Symphony Orchestra for one well-attended performance.[33]

The reopened Elks Opera House of 1902 erased much of the Tabor Opera House's legacy. The outside of the theatre was mostly untouched, but a new, larger stage was installed, the ornate proscenium was replaced by a plain, square frame, and dressing rooms were rearranged below the stage. In the auditorium, the walnut paneling was removed, as were the once-handsome opera seats. They were replaced by smaller wooden chairs, which allowed the seating capacity to rise to 1,000. Ticket prices, at 10 and 20 cents, were a fraction of those charged during the Tabor's heyday.[34]

The refurbishing increased attendance for a time, persuading Anna Held and John Philip Sousa to appear, among other stars. Vaudeville played every night the house was not booked for something grander. The opera house settled into a quiet decline. Its last engagement as a full-time theatre was in 1925, when the musical *Abe's Irish Rose* was produced. The Tabor's opulent next-door neighbor, the Clarendon Hotel, was torn down in the 1930s. Two decades later the opera house was sold again, this time to a retired schoolteacher from Minnesota named Florence Hollister, who wanted to save the building from demolition. Mrs. Hollister restored Tabor's name to the opera house and attempted to rescue it from decay. At her death, Mrs. Hollister passed the Tabor on to her daughter, Evelyn Furman, who maintains the theatre today with help from her daughter and son-in-

Leadville's Tabor Opera House stage in 1933. The stage has been enlarged and the apron extended, and the austere proscenium bears almost no resemblance to its appearance fifty years earlier.
PHOTO COURTESY DENVER PUBLIC LIBRARY, WESTERN HISTORY COLLECTION, IRA B. CURRENT, X-187

law, Sharon and Bill Bland. The ceiling frescoes and paneling have been painted over, but Mrs. Furman has reinstalled many of the original Andrews opera seats, which the Elks had stored in the attic years earlier. A portrait of Tabor hangs to the left of the stage, a gift from the Tabor Grand in Denver when it was torn down.

A dusty shabbiness hangs over the building today. Mrs. Furman's taped voice repeats the story of the old opera house as visitors wander its aisles and staircases, sit on the original wooden benches in the balcony, and poke through the threadbare dressing rooms below the stage. The single trap door still operates, as it did when Houdini used it; the original light box hangs off-stage. Draperies no longer grace the skeletons of the once-lavish boxes, and the carpet is well worn. Melodrama and summer theatre companies have staged performances in the old playhouse through the years.

That the Tabor Opera House has survived this long, not succumbing to fire, demolition crews, or benign neglect, is a small miracle. There is a certain charm in the unrestored old building, but time has taken its toll. For many years, Mrs. Furman maintained the opera house solely from the income generated by visitors, refusing all grants and outside help. At last in 1995, she and a group of townspeople called the Leadville Coalition successfully applied to the State Historical Fund for monies to stabilize the walls, replace the roof, and begin restoration of the exterior. The state's generous response came at a propitious time, injecting sufficient capital to save the building from decaying so far as to be unsalvageable. With the establishment of the Tabor Opera House Preservation Foundation, the theatre has embarked on a rehabilitation process coinciding with the growing popularity of historic tourism. There are promising signs that this historic landmark, the earliest surviving example of Tabor's steadfast commitment to Colorado, may live long enough to see the state and its residents respond in kind to his munificence.

ASPEN

Wheeler Opera House

OPENED: APRIL 23, 1889

CURRENTLY A THEATRE AND CONCERT HALL

West of Leadville, on the other side of the Continental Divide, sits Aspen. Both communities owe their existence to silver, which brought the people and the wealth that made the towns possible. Like Leadville, Aspen has a historic opera house built by the generosity of another early, wealthy resident, Jerome Byron Wheeler. The two theatres are similar in size and date from the same era. But while Tabor was a long-time Colorado resident, the cosmopolitan Wheeler called many places home and never put down roots in Aspen. And while both were shrewd businessmen who capitalized spectacularly on their luck, Wheeler entered the game a wealthy man.

Born in Troy, New York, in 1841, Wheeler was a successful flour merchant when he made his most fateful move: he married Harriet Macy Valentine, niece of the founder of Macy's, New York's largest department store. When all but one of the Macy partners died in quick succession, Wheeler was asked to become a partner, securing his fortune, which he speedily combined with his own impressive entrepreneurial talents.[35]

Wheeler came to the Colorado spa town of Manitou Springs in the early 1880s, seeking a healthier climate for his wife. Although significant silver strikes had made Aspen a promising mining camp, its isolation had hampered development. Alerted to Aspen's possibilities, Wheeler saw an opportunity, invested in mining property, and then bought and completed a languishing smelter on Castle Creek, finally giving Aspen miners the ability to process their own ore. Freed from the necessity of hauling unsmelted ore to Leadville by mule, Aspen mining grew quickly.[36]

All Colorado mining towns started out with a few hardy souls prospecting in primitive camps, but Aspen had city aspirations from the start. Once it was incorporated in 1880, early civic leaders made the establishment of schools and churches a priority. A chapter of the Temperance Union was founded in 1881, reflecting residents' concerns with building a clean-living town. By 1885, with over 4,000 residents, Aspen had only twenty-six saloons, as opposed to rowdy Leadville's eighty.[37] City fathers also decreed that unseemly behavior would be confined to a strictly bounded red-light district, known to locals as "The Row."

As Aspen evolved, so did its entertainment. Early tent theatres gave way to variety theatres and traveling troupe houses such as the Rink Opera House, a combination theatre and roller skating rink. Although it seems an unlikely combination now, rink theatres were common in the period; by 1885, Aspen's had the distinction of being the only building in town with gas lighting. Seating 500, it allowed early Aspen residents to see touring productions at modest prices.[38]

Like other Colorado mining communities, Aspen's stature was increased by the coming of the railroad. On November 2, 1887, the narrow-gauge Denver & Rio Grande arrived to great celebration: the town's bands played all night, a banquet and grand ball were held for Aspen's elite, and free drinks were the rule at area saloons. Shortly thereafter, the standard-gauge Colorado Midland, backed by Jerome Wheeler, steamed into town on December 18, 1887. Its arrival was possible through the engineering of the spectacular Hagerman Tunnel across the Continental Divide at a cost of two million dollars.[39] The coming of not one, but two, railroads made it much easier for traveling theatre companies to get to Aspen. Road shows became more frequent, but they seldom included the best touring companies, due to the lack of a first-class theatre. Some troupes, as this reviewer writes, must have been mediocre at best:

> *The dramatic atrocity [witnessed by] amusement seekers of Aspen . . . made its escape via the Midland on Sunday and it is to be inflicted on the unfortunate people of Pueblo tonight. As a failure the company are a histrionic climax and the remainder of the circuit is entitled to heart felt sympathy.* [40]

Into Aspen's theatrical plight stepped Jerome Wheeler. He thrilled Aspenites by announcing in February 1888 that he would provide not only a fine new bank building for the city, but that it would also house a "public hall, complete with stage fixtures."[41]

As befitted Aspen's most prominent investor, the bank building and opera house were conceived on a grand scale for a city of 6,000 residents. Wheeler hired W. J. Edbrooke, architect of the lavish Tabor Grand Opera House in Denver, to design his building. The site, at the corner of Hyman Avenue and Mill Street, was in the center of the town's commercial district. The red sandstone and brick edifice became the largest brick building in downtown.

An early, undated engraving of the Wheeler Opera House, Aspen. The J. B. Wheeler Bank occupied the first floor of the red sandstone and brick building, and the opera house resided on the third.
COURTESY ASPEN HISTORICAL SOCIETY COLLECTIONS

The structure opened in stages, with mishaps along the way. After construction began in June 1888, residents began to comment by autumn that the east wall appeared to be buckling. Despite assurances from the construction superintendent, Edbrooke declared that the wall had to come down and be almost entirely rebuilt. During the reconstruction, a scaffold full of workmen fell, injuring four. The accident prompted Aspenites to begin construction of a city hospital.[43]

Finally, on March 20, 1889, the building's first business opened its doors to suitably impressed townsfolk. The J. B. Wheeler Bank featured a marble entryway, handsome cherry furniture, heavy carpets, and the latest in bank vaults. Other occupants followed, all as elegant as the bank. A little over a month after the bank opened, on April 23, the third-floor Wheeler Opera House was completed at a cost of $125,000. Using the Hyman Avenue entrance, theatregoers entered the auditorium after mounting a wide staircase. The brilliantly lit house accommodated 800 people and was divided between parquet and balcony levels, both of which were outfitted with opera chairs covered in brown morocco leather. Reviewers remarked particularly about the stylishness of the seating, contrasting it with the uncomfortable straw-filled seats at the Rink Opera House. The aisles were carpeted in red and led to the two semicircular proscenium boxes that flanked the stage and seated five each. The gold plush upholstery on the mahogany chairs blended with the gold wallpapered boxes, each of which was topped by a blue fan-shaped vault trimmed with silver stars. Directly in front of the stage was a small area for a handful of musicians.[43]

The Wheeler was one of the first theatres in the state to use electric lighting. Onstage, this allowed a greater range of lighting effects, while the auditorium was brightly lit by a brass chandelier. With three dozen opalescent glass shades, it hung from the center of the frescoed ceiling and formed, as an *Aspen Daily Times* reviewer wrote, "the crowning glory of this beautiful house."[44]

Commodious as the auditorium was, the stage area had limitations. The stage measured 50 feet wide by a scant 26 feet deep; its height, 25 feet, allowed for little storage of scenery. Clearly, Jerome Wheeler had built a bank that housed a theatre and not the other way around. Still, there was an ample collection of fifteen sets of scenery, costing $8,000,

The stage and boxes of the Wheeler Opera House as they appeared shortly after the opening in April 1889. The Wheeler was one of the first in the state to be built with electric lighting.
GENERAL 1723, ARCHIVES, UNIVERSITY OF COLORADO AT BOULDER LIBRARIES

and a drop curtain designed by Charles Graham of *Harper's Weekly* and Homer Emons. Interestingly, it depicted the "Brooklyn Bridge viewed from the New York side of the East River," perhaps a nod to the theatre's New York-born owner.[45]

Because space was limited, props and scenery were stored elsewhere and brought in through a door behind the stage. Nearby was a staircase that descended to the eight dressing rooms, all of which had hot and cold running water. An 1896 theatrical guide states there was a single trap door in the center of the stage floor.[46] The stage was probably also outfitted with a treadmill.

A first-class theatre demanded first-class management, and Wheeler hired a New York theatre manager, Ralph A. Weill, to run his opera house. Weill divided his time between Aspen and New York, trumpeting the glories of the new theatre in both places while arranging for its opening. He met with Peter McCourt to discuss bookings for the Wheeler on the Silver Circuit, and, indeed, the opening performances were given by Conried's English Comic Opera Company, then touring for McCourt.[47]

Encouraged by Weill's publicity, anticipation in Aspen rose as the opening grew nearer. Descriptions of the new theatre were run in the newspaper, along with a synopsis of the opening-night opera. A band greeted the arriving company at the train station. As an enticement to those less interested in opera than assessing well-turned ankles, Weill arranged for a fencing contest between the ladies of the visiting opera company, offering a purse of $150 on opening night.[48] With excitement running high, both the manager and residents were astonished to hear that the theatre's patron, Jerome Wheeler, would not attend the opening. Plans for a fête in his honor were canceled, and townspeople had their hopes dashed that Mr. Wheeler would ever take up residence in Aspen. His indifference to the theatre is telling; not for the last time would the Wheeler Opera House suffer from its namesake's neglect.

Despite Wheeler's absence, the opening on April 23, 1889, was a success. The house was filled with elegantly attired residents, and the *Aspen Daily Times* reviewer noted that the air was redolent with perfume from the scented satin programs presented to the ladies at the door. Each also received a complimentary bottle of perfume. The reviewer continued that the opening entertainment, *The King's Fool*, "included a cast of eighty artists and offered bewilderingly beautiful marches, dazzling electrical effects, and enchanting music."[49]

The Conried Opera Company performed only twice before moving on to other Silver Circuit stops. Despite the glitter surrounding the

The souvenir program for the opening night of the Wheeler Opera House was printed on pastel satin.

opening, not all theatregoers were impressed by the quality of the production they had seen. An editorial run in the *Aspen Daily Times* the day
after the Conried Company left expressed a desire to mark the
Wheeler's opening with something truly memorable, such as an appearance by the great tragedians Booth and Barrett, scheduled to perform in
Denver the following week:

> *Can't they be induced to come over here so that we can have the
> Wheeler Opera House opened over again? . . . They would draw
> packed houses in a two nights' engagement, and the people of Aspen
> would feel that their opera house had been properly dedicated. There
> is no use in attempting to disguise the disappointment that followed
> the performance of the third rate troupe that has just been here, so let
> us have something standard.*[50]

The writer of the editorial had hit upon a problem that was to dog
the Wheeler throughout its early history: because it was a small town
reached with difficulty through the mountains, Aspen managers had
persistent difficulty persuading first-rate performers to book there. Weill
stated that he had to guarantee the Conried $2,500 to open the house,
a practice many theatre managers tried to avoid, and surprising considering that it was the much-anticipated opening entertainment.[51] Weill
may have assumed that Peter McCourt would simply add Aspen to the
Silver Circuit's regular stops, but such was not the case. In its first season, the Wheeler averaged only two or three traveling companies each
month, and the rest of the time it relied on home talent, local meetings,
and church services to keep the lights on.

Perhaps out of frustration with the situation, Weill abruptly resigned
two months after the Wheeler opened. A month later, the property manager, Robert J. Cutler, was promoted to take Weill's place. Shortly thereafter, on July 15, 1889, Helena Modjeska, the great classical actress,
appeared with her company for two nights in *As You Like It* and *Adrienne
Lecouvreur*, to glowing reviews. The appreciation was mutual, for Modjeska
stated in an interview that she was "particularly pleased with the evening's
audience" and "had never played [Rosalind] before a house that more
quickly recognized the fine points of the play."[52]

Cutler's management was popular with Aspen residents, although
like Weill, he also found that bookings were hard to come by without
guaranteeing companies large sums to appear. Nevertheless, he arranged
for the popular Irish character actor Edward Harrigan to open the fall
season with *Old Lavender*, reportedly drawing an immense audience that

was delighted by his musical features. Other entertainers to appear during the Wheeler's first year included the venerable Milton and Dolly Nobles Company for two nights and Aspen favorite Patti Rosa with her company for one night. Of her performance in *Margery Daw*, the newspaper reviewer wrote, "The little lady has struck a gold mine and her silver mining friends wish her much success."[53]

The number of bookings increased through Cutler's tenure, as did the variety of entertainment, including opera companies, minstrel shows, a little Shakespeare, and the perennially popular *Uncle Tom's Cabin*. Despite his popularity with local theatregoers, Cutler announced his intention to return to New York in April 1890, ostensibly because of his own poor health and that of one of his daughters. His replacement, the enterprising W. B. Cochran, was chosen by Jerome Wheeler from the rank of his bank employees, another indication that Wheeler was largely unconcerned with theatre operations. Cochran turned into a credible manager, however, despite having to split his time between demands at the bank, and later, at the Hotel Jerome. He brought in a number of highly regarded entertainers and troupes, while conceding that he could fill a house for only one night. To the irritation of Aspen theatregoers, this restriction eventually led troupes to cut the length of their performances so that they could make the late train out of town.

One of Cochran's innovations to increase his audience was to capitalize on the popular trains that carried Aspen dwellers to Glenwood Springs on weekends to bathe in the hot springs. By offering Glenwood Springs residents special train rates, he enticed them to Aspen and the Wheeler, bolstering its sagging attendance. This arrangement worked especially well when one of the rare two-night stands was planned, as when Robert Mantell appeared in *Othello* and *Monbars* in September 1890.[54]

A number of first-rate attractions came to the Wheeler in 1890, ranging from Augustin Daly's New York touring company to popular actress Effie Ellsler. The original Broadway cast of Bronson Howard's *Shenandoah* appeared to an especially large house. The *Aspen Daily Times* reviewer reported that "at times the excitement was painfully intense." He also found the ladies of the company to be "clever" and "very fair to look upon." With unintentional humor, the reviewer stated that the depiction of the "roar of guns and wounded and dying men can only be told by those who had the pleasure of witnessing this performance."[55]

In June, fans of the "manly art" saw middleweight boxing champion Jack Dempsey, the "Nonpareil," dispatch an opponent while reportedly remaining "cool as a cucumber."[56] Although appreciative of boxing exhibitions and battle scenes, audiences at the Wheeler were more genteel than those at other Western mining towns. Largely well behaved and well dressed, theatregoers expected to see only wholesome entertainment. Reviewers were usually quick to point out any vulgarity and condemn it forcefully, as when Turner's English Girls Company presented *Cleopatra* in February 1893. "Simply Rotten," sniffed the headline. The reviewer complained that the production belonged in the "beer halls of Cincinnati and the dance halls of State Street, Leadville. The men who left their families at home were well pleased."[57]

Nevertheless, the prospect of an act with ladies in revealing costumes often drew well, although it was seldom advertised as such. The Turner's English Girls prompted the *Aspen Daily Times* reviewer to note that "all the bald heads in Aspen answered to roll call . . . at the Wheeler Opera House last night. They were pretty well bunched in the front rows."[58]

Even as early as 1891, tendencies emerged that increasingly characterized the Wheeler and its audiences. In addition to moving almost exclusively to one-night stands, visiting companies got smaller and programs got lighter: Shakespeare was performed only six times in the Wheeler's early heyday, and the theatre gradually came to depend more on locally produced shows and meetings to supplement engagements by touring groups. Home talent entertainments usually were benefits for church groups, although sometimes they were given for needy townspeople, such as those held for widows whose husbands had been lost in mining accidents or avalanches. Various religious groups used the theatre, ranging from the Christ Episcopal Church, which held services there until its building was completed, to the 1889 Yom Kippur service for Jewish residents. On several occasions miners held meetings at the Wheeler to discuss silver prices, mining concerns, and how to entice investors to Aspen. There were annual Memorial Day observances and political rallies and conventions. In 1890, there were two mysterious lectures given "for men only," entitled "Errors of Life" and "Specific Diseases."

Managers Cutler and Cochran realized the importance of sharing the Wheeler with the locals, although the prospects of making money with home talent benefits were slim. Both unhappily discovered that turning a profit at the Wheeler was not easy, even with big names as draws. An especially large guarantee was promised to the highly regarded Bostonians for their one appearance in Suppé's opera *Fatinitza* on March 13, 1891. Cochran was forced to raise prices to cover the expense, but mercifully ticket sales were brisk and the local reviewer wrote, "the musical people of Aspen had a treat that they will not forget for a long time."[59]

Other headliners came to the Wheeler in 1891, including Kate Claxton. Miss Claxton appeared in her signature role of Louise from *The Two Orphans* on the fifteenth anniversary of the disastrous New York theatre fire, which killed hundreds in 1876 during her performance of the same play. In order to hold at abeyance what the reviewer called "an overpowering sense of impending calamity felt by many of the theatergoers," the manager thoughtfully had firefighters stationed before the footlights, should disaster strike. It didn't, but it is not coincidental that this publicity minded move swelled the size of the audience. The review ran the next day under the headline, "Claxton, but no fire."[60]

Patti Rosa, billed as the Female Elk, in observance of her status as the only female member of that fraternal order, returned on February 18, 1891. Because she was a favorite in Aspen, theatregoers indulgently overlooked the roughness of her character in *Imp*, although newspaper reviews made it clear the part was not as wholesome as usual Wheeler fare.[61] Touring spectaculars, minstrel shows, vaudeville, lectures, and benefits rounded out the year.

The Wheeler hosted two of the nation's most famous touring groups in 1892: the Charles Frohman company came on two occasions, followed by Haverly's Minstrels. Although bookings were plentiful, lackluster troupes still made their way to Aspen, as when the Kimball Opera Company arrived in March. "[A] company of some forty very ordinary people, so far as talent is concerned, appeared . . . to a much better house than they deserved," the newspaper account went. Finding the acts vulgar and the jokes hoary with age, the reviewer also questioned the claims the company made in its advertising: "The two carloads of special scenery was left in the Rio Grande yards, if they had it."[62]

There were ominous signs on the nation's financial horizon, and with a steeply falling silver market, ticket prices were cut in March to boost sales. Although not apparent then, the glory days of the high-flying silver barons were over.

Despite the uncertain economic future, manager W. B. Cochran believed the time was right to launch his own opera company to provide a season of summer opera for patrons of the Wheeler as well as other cities on the Silver Circuit. The decision led to his downfall. Drawing heavily (and possibly illegally) on the profits of the Wheeler to hire and outfit his fledgling company, Cochran spent liberally. Unfortunately, his female star, Emma Berg, failed to excite opera-goers, and productions drew only moderate crowds. Cochran resigned his post as manager of the Wheeler to devote himself to the company, but he reached the end of the line, both literally and figuratively, when the troupe arrived in Salt Lake City. It disbanded there, and several days later a warrant was issued for Cochran's arrest by the Wheeler's new managers, who were at last aware of his ruinous spending at the opera house's expense.[63]

In disarray, the Wheeler's offerings were scant throughout the rest of 1892, which was hardly surprising, considering that the new manager was another bank employee with no experience in running a theatre. Twenty-five-year-old James Ryan managed to bring in only a couple of touring groups a month, while locals filled in the rest of the time. Audiences shrank as Aspen continued to reel from the downturn in the silver market and from epidemics of diphtheria and scarlet fever. As silver prices continued to fall, theatre became a luxury few could afford.

The Silver Panic of 1893 and the repeal of the Sherman Silver Act in November sealed the fate of Aspen and the Wheeler. The theatre was mortgaged in the spring of that year. By July, the Wheeler Bank was closed, as was every mine in Aspen. Many left town and virtually all businesses stopped. Loyal to the end, both Patti Rosa and Effie Ellsler made appearances in 1894, but other offerings were infrequent and forgettable. Almost five years to the day after the Wheeler's glittering

Musicians and minstrels appearing on the stage of the Wheeler Opera House during the 1904–5 season.

opening, the theatre closed. In the succeeding years, it was used occasionally to show moving pictures and, less often, for locally produced live entertainment.

Worse was to come. After operating fitfully for years, the theatre suffered two suspicious and devastating fires within a week of each other in 1912, destroying all the stage properties, scenery, stage, and boxes. The third floor was boarded up, a blackened ruin, and forgotten.

In the late 1940s, fortune at last smiled on the Wheeler. Walter Paepcke, a Chicago manufacturer, undertook restoration of the theatre as part of his plan to rebuild the city of Aspen into a cultural and intellectual mecca. With Bauhaus-trained artist and architect Herbert Bayer, Walter and Elizabeth Paepcke staged the Goethe Bicentennial Convocation in July 1949. They invited luminaries from many disciplines, from Albert Schweitzer to Thornton Wilder, with musicians Artur Rubenstein and the entire Minneapolis Symphony Orchestra, to take part. The Aspen Institute and The Aspen Music Festival grew out of the Convocation, and the Wheeler became central to their well-being. Reopened with the most austere of stages and plainest of auditoriums (the audience sat on backless wooden benches), the Wheeler eventually underwent a renovation that restored many of its original features. A rich mix of actors, musicians, and film scholars appeared at the Wheeler as the Paepckes's plans for Aspen became reality. Grand opera was staged every summer, including works by Darius Milhaud and Benjamin Britten, who were there to witness them. Film study took over the Wheeler exclusively by 1969, when a nightly film series was initiated, running until 1982.

By that time, increasingly prosperous Aspen residents had rallied around the Wheeler. Through a municipal real estate transfer tax, another major renovation was undertaken. The theatre had its grand reopening on May 24, 1984, after an expenditure of $4.5 million dollars. Looking much like it must have when it opened almost a century before, down to a reproduction of the Brooklyn Bridge drop curtain, the improved Wheeler boasted state-of-the-art lighting, sound, and projection capacities (an improvement over the broom closet that was used when the film studies program began in the 1950s), and redesigned stage space. New seating was installed to accommodate today's larger patrons, resulting in a capacity of 489, about two-thirds of what the original house could hold. A convertible orchestra pit was added; the bank lobby on the first floor became the theatre lobby.

The opening gala of May 1984 included a production of George Bernard Shaw's *Arms and the Man* by the Denver Center Theatre

Company, dance by Moses Pendleton and his MOMIX company, a joint concert by James Levine at the piano and cellist Lynn Harrell, and a screening of 1928's *The Wind*, introduced by its star, Lillian Gish. With its funding assured by the transfer tax, the Wheeler has made performance space available to community groups and non-profits at minimal expense, while continuing to offer venues for new artists and musical plays. A magnet for artists everywhere, the Wheeler has hosted a wide range of performers, from Lily Tomlin to John Denver to Wynton Marsalis. The annual Aspen Filmfest has premiered such award-winners as *The Piano, The Crying Game*, and *Blue*.

To celebrate the opera house's hundredth anniversary in 1989, Harry Connick, Jr., performed, followed by a concert with returning favorite Lynn Harrell. Continuing the tradition that marked it from its earliest days, the Wheeler still hosts a vibrant mix of home talent shows alternating with nationally known performers, surely equaling the range and fame of those it knew in the 1890s.

Wheeler Opera House Executive Director Robert Murray concludes, "The Wheeler is glorious to look at, versatile in its uses, and very, very busy. . . . [It] has been an enormous morale booster for a self-critical town. It has brought opportunity and inspiration, wrapped in velvet and adorned with silver stars, to artists and to audiences. It illustrates to the world what imagination, taste and daring can accomplish. Of what the Real and the Fabled Aspen is capable."[64]

CHAPTER FIVE

COLORADO SPRINGS AND PUEBLO

COLORADO SPRINGS

Colorado Springs Opera House

OPENED: APRIL 18, 1881

CONVERTED TO A MOVIE THEATRE: 1918

REMODELED FOR COMMERCIAL USE: 1928

CURRENTLY HOUSES SMALL BARS

AND NIGHTCLUBS

By the time ground was broken for its opera house in July 1880, Colorado Springs was already an established theatre town. Founded on July 31, 1871, by General William Jackson Palmer, the "Fountain Colony" from its inception was intended as a tourist, cultural, and health center, "the cosmopolitan oasis of the American West."[1] Its reputation for beauty, wealth, and refinement—which, in Palmer's mind, translated to British culture—lured tourists from both the East Coast and overseas, and the new resort town readily adopted the nicknames "Newport in the Rockies" and "Little London." Meanwhile, Palmer sought to attract residents of "good moral character and strict temperance,"[2] befitting a town with no saloons or liquor for sale. A decade after establishing Colorado Springs, and the Denver & Rio Grande

Railroad that made it possible, Palmer could boast of a growing town (population 4,500) that was already running out of hotel rooms to accommodate its fashionable tourists.

Theatre was an integral part of the Colorado Springs cultural scene during its first decade, the need being met by a series of second-floor public halls. The best of these, City Hall, was built in 1876, a structure approximately 50 feet square with a stage only 20 by 10 feet. Nevertheless, it presented touring companies such as George Rignold's "grand opera house troupe" appearing in Shakespeare's *Henry V* on May 29, 1878. The backstage area was so cramped that only one actor at a time could dress and put on makeup, and the confines were made even more precarious by the appearance of King Henry's white horse, Crispin, who had somehow been coaxed up a flight of stairs. However, the actors accepted the rough-and-ready surroundings with good humor. When the performance began and King Henry (played by Rignold) ordered the French emissaries, "Begone," he added in an undertone, "But I don't know where the devil you'll go to!" At one point, overcome by the absurdity of the setting, Rignold stopped in the middle of a soliloquy and addressed the packed audience of 200, "This is really too ridiculous, ladies and gentlemen. You must be content simply with the beautiful words of Shakespeare, for I've nothing more to offer you." But he did have more to offer: later in the play, as Henry was rallying his troops, he accidentally impaled the royal flagstaff in the low ceiling, where it stuck fast.[3]

Better times were fast approaching, and in less than three years, Colorado Springs had a splendid facility to offer its audiences and visiting performers. Irving Howbert and his partners at the First National Bank, Benjamin Crowell and Joseph F. Humphrey, having made a fortune together in the Robert E. Lee silver mine at Leadville, decided to invest $80,000 in a new opera house. Their goal was to erect an elegant and lavish theatre, one that would compare favorably with—and be completed before—the Tabor Grand Opera House under construction in Denver. It would offer only first-class theatre with no variety-hall or saloon entertainment. The building, designed by A. C. Willard and Company of Colorado Springs, stood next to the First National Bank at 18–20 North Tejon Street, on lots owned by the financiers.

It was an impressive structure of pressed brick, black mortar, and saffron-colored sandstone that nevertheless gave little hint of its decorous and fanciful interior. The stage was 55 feet wide and 30 feet deep, set behind a magnificent, gold-decorated proscenium arch 24 feet wide and 24 feet high. A lovely drop curtain showed a Venetian scene accompanied by the words "Nil sine numine"—nothing without Providence.

Exterior of the Colorado Springs Opera House (date unknown). The façade featured pressed brick and black mortar, accented by saffron–colored sandstone. COLORADO SPRINGS PIONEERS MUSEUM

(According to Marshall Sprague, Colorado Springs historian, Benjamin Crowell translated the Latin as "No sign of a new mine."[4]) The stage allowed sufficient room for scenery and special effects, with a height of 36 feet from stage floor to rigging loft. Lighting was provided by over 261 gas jets and an elegant dome chandelier, which revealed the rich colors and polished brass of the interior. Next to the stage, four private boxes were resplendent with carpets, silk plush drapery, and hangings of gold and lace. The auditorium seated 800 people and an orchestra in an area 49 feet from curtain line to back wall and 55 feet from side to side. Playgoers in the parquet (today's orchestra level), parquet circle, and balcony sat on individual chairs upholstered in silk maroon plush. Those who could not afford the $1.50 tickets in the parquet or $1.00 in the balcony paid 50 cents to sit on uncomfortable benches in the gallery (nicknamed the "Garden of the Gods"), from where they could not see the entire stage.

Engraving of the interior of the Colorado Springs Opera House,
c. 1881, showing the theatre's decorative ceiling and upper auditorium.

Parquet, parquet circle, and balcony, Colorado Springs Opera House,
1881. The upper gallery (nicknamed "the Garden of the Gods") is cast in
shadow, and playgoers sitting there had to endure wooden benches and a
restricted view of the stage.

For the opening production, the legendary theatre manager Jack Langrishe and his partner, Pierce, engaged Maude Granger and her company, which had been performing at the short-lived Sixteenth Street Theatre in Denver. Unfortunately Miss Granger chose *Camille* for the premiere, a highly unpopular choice with the local citizenry because the heroine dies of tuberculosis in the final act, while Colorado Springs took pride in its restorative climate and reputation as "the sanitarium of the world." "For a house full of consumptives to see a poor creature fade away with this fell disease is not desirable," a correspondent wrote to the newspaper. "People go to such places for recreation and amusement; not to be reminded of their latter end. The clergy are supposed to take charge of that part of the programme."[5] Some have alleged that local businessmen wanted to alter the final act so that Camille would be revived by the favorable Colorado Springs air, a suggestion flatly

Set stage with ornate patent opera seats, c. 1881.
PHOTO COURTESY DENVER PUBLIC LIBRARY, WESTERN HISTORY COLLECTION, H. S. POLEY, P-1848

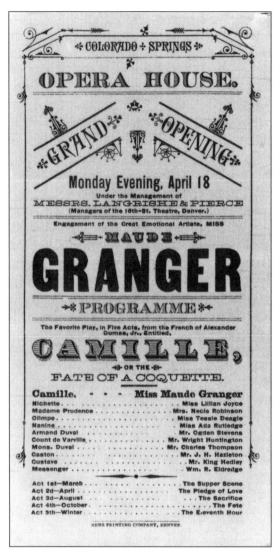

COLORADO SPRINGS

OPERA HOUSE.

GRAND OPENING

Monday Evening, April 18

Under the Management of

MESSRS. LANGRISHE & PIERCE

(Managers of the 16th-St. Theatre, Denver.)

Engagement of the Great Emotional Artiste, MISS

MAUDE

GRANGER

PROGRAMME

The Favorite Play, in Five Acts, from the French of Alexander Dumas, Jr., Entitled,

CAMILLE,

OR THE

FATE OF A COQUETTE.

Camille.	- - -	**Miss Maude Granger**
Nichette		Miss Lillian Joyce
Madame Prudence		Mrs. Necia Robinson
Olimpe		Miss Tessie Deagle
Nanine		Miss Ada Rutledge
Armand Duval		Mr. Ogden Stevens
Count de Varville		Mr. Wright Huntington
Mons. Duval		Mr. Charles Thompson
Gaston		Mr. J. H. Hazleton
Gustave		Mr. King Hedley
Messenger		Wm. R. Eldredge

Act 1st—March	The Supper Scene
Act 2d—April	The Pledge of Love
Act 3d—August	The Sacrifice
Act 4th—October	The Fete
Act 5th—Winter	The Eleventh Hour

NEWS PRINTING COMPANY, DENVER.

Opening night program, Colorado Springs Opera House, April 18, 1881.

rejected by Miss Granger, who tore the revised scripts to pieces. (This altercation actually occurred, but it was thirty years later, when "the Divine" Sarah Bernhardt played the role.) From that time on, *Camille* was thought to be an unlucky play for Colorado Springs. Manager Simeon Nye could not bear to watch the Bernhardt production, but nervously walked up and down Tejon Street during the performance.

Opening night of April 18, 1881, was a glittering society affair. As fashionable theatregoers arrived in carriages, they walked under carved, white-oak arches into a vestibule lit by a polished brass lantern, along a hallway decorated with ash and black-walnut wainscot, and into a lobby with grand staircases leading to the balcony. The stairway newels were constructed of black walnut, and each supported a bronze knight holding a flambeau. As they took their seats, patrons received a white-satin, souvenir program recording the cast and management in gold lettering. Reviewers marveled at "the handsomest theatre of its size in America"[6] and praised both the production and the beauty of Maude Granger. The only flaw in an otherwise unqualified success occurred on the second night of *Camille*, in the final act:

> *The couch upon which the actress was to make her ascent into the starry regions happened to be poorly constructed, while the actress herself was rather portly. So, when…breathing her last breaths of this sordid existence, Camille saw visions of a new world, the cot gave way, and instead of finding herself securely housed in another sphere the actress found herself in an ungraceful position on the floor. The climax, however, was capped when Miss Granger, not knowing the curtain had been raised for her to answer a call, uttered forth a volly [sic] of abuse upon the stage manager in hearing of the entire audience, in terms not at all conducive to her good reputation.*[7]

Audiences apparently overlooked Miss Granger's indiscretion, since receipts for her seven performances totaled $1,570, by far the largest box-office take of the first season.[8]

The stage manager who was the recipient of Maude Granger's ire may well have been Simeon Nash Nye, the most significant of all the names associated with the Colorado Springs Opera House in terms of both influence and longevity. A recent arrival from Ohio, the thirty-three-year-old Nye was initially responsible for preparing and mounting the scenery and furnishings on stage. But ten months after the opening, on February 18, 1882, he was appointed theatre manager, a position he would maintain for almost all of the

Maude Granger (1851?-1929), taken about the time she opened the Colorado Springs Opera House.
COURTESY OF THE HUNTINGTON LIBRARY, SAN MARINO, CALIFORNIA

next thirty-two years. Except for immediately dismissing the theatre orchestra and hiring a new one, he continued the policies of his predecessors, Joseph H. Hazleton and A. S. Welch, in establishing the new opera house on the burgeoning "Colorado Circuit." Nye understood that Colorado Springs could not support a permanent company but was more or less a one-night stand, and its survival depended on booking touring companies like Maude Granger's that were already performing at the Tabor Opera House in Leadville or the Tabor Grand in Denver. Fortunately, engaging such companies was relatively easy because the railroad route from Denver to Leadville at that time went through Colorado Springs.

At first there was no set itinerary, and the enterprising Nye soon began to manage the tours of certain performing groups or individuals. His first venture, in April 1882, was the lecture tour of Oscar Wilde across Colorado. On April 14, Nye brought Wilde to Colorado Springs to deliver a lecture on "Art Decoration," Wilde appearing in a black velvet dress coat, lace collar and cuffs, knee breeches, silk stockings, and shoes with sparkling buckles. Attendees were few but attentive, "and occasionally when he would give expression to a brilliant thought or idea a murmur of applause would pass through the audience."[9]

The following month, Nye arranged for another "first:" the appearance of famous Shakespearean actor Lawrence Barrett, in *Hamlet*, on May 27. Clearly, Colorado Springs had come a long way from the travesty of George Rignold's *Henry V* just four years earlier. Now a reviewer could concentrate on the fine points of a performance rather than the former inadequacies of the stage:

> *His Hamlet is strong, passionate and intellectual rather than gentle, self-controlled and philosophical. It is not the Hamlet one sees in reading Shakespeare…. The play shows the wonderful action of Barrett which in its lightning speed and transition gives such force to passionate utterance. There has certainly been no such powerful acting in our opera house as that of last night.*[10]

The production was so successful that Nye immediately signed Barrett to a return engagement the following year.

By 1883, Nye had established so many theatre contacts that he was able to announce a full season's program in the newspapers, although plans were always subject to change. Generally he booked minstrel shows, opera companies, an annual production of *Uncle Tom's Cabin,* and a wide variety of plays, interspersed with occasional lectures and concerts. For example, on April 5, 1884, the well-known actress Kate Claxton performed in a sensational melodrama, *The Sea of Ice,* in which she played a courageous mother who saves her child by leaping from one "Startling Ice Floe" to another. She also demonstrated great presence of mind when a sudden gust of wind blew the theatre doors open and the dusty air was mistaken for smoke, precipitating that most dreaded cry of alarm: "Fire!" She managed to avert a panic by calming the audience, and the play continued.[11] A less happy outcome occurred after the performance of Annie Eva Fay, the "materializing medium" and "mysterious phenomenon," on August 14, 1881:

> *Annie Eva Fay and her assistants, whoever they may be, left the city at an early hour yesterday morning leaving several unsettled accounts and we understand that they make this their practice wherever they go. Among others who suffered was the dressmaker who provided the medium with the dress which she wore on the stage Sunday night. What advancement can spiritualism make in this or any other land if such impostors as Annie Eva Fay be allowed to travel the country and impose upon the people?*[12]

Colorado Springs also produced talent of its own. Lon Chaney, a Colorado Springs native later known as "The Man of a Thousand Faces," began his career in 1902 as a prop boy earning 25 cents a night at the opera house, although he never performed there.

Throughout the 1880s, the success of the Colorado Springs Opera House can be directly attributed to Nye's increasing influence in the Colorado theatre scene. In addition to his duties in Colorado Springs, he became provisional manager at the Tabor Grand in Denver as well as new theatres in Trinidad and Salida. He continued to organize and oversee the circuit that ran between these towns, booked the companies (sometimes traveling to Chicago or St. Louis to recruit them), and accompanied them on their tours. A turning point in his career occurred in 1884 when he refused Horace Tabor's offer to become permanent manager of the Tabor Grand, and the position was given instead to Tabor's inexperienced brother-in-law, Peter McCourt. Although Nye continued to operate somewhat independently, McCourt gradually became a more powerful influence, culminating in his establishment of the Silver Circuit in June 1889. McCourt was also instrumental in keeping the Colorado Springs Opera House financially solvent when, in August 1885, attendance dropped and the theatre closed amid rumors that it was to be turned into a hotel. McCourt rallied local businessmen to support the theatre, and a new season commenced the following month.

Some of the stars who appeared in Colorado Springs in the 1880s included James O'Neill in his famous performance of *The Count of*

Monte Cristo, Lotta Crabtree ("the darling of the mining camps and the West") in *Musette*, Minnie Maddern in *Caprice*, and, on June 10, 1887, Lillie Langtry in *A Wife's Peril*. To accommodate such stars and their large touring productions, and draw larger audiences with a more attractive and comfortable auditorium, Nye undertook to renovate the opera house in the summer of 1891 by adding four additional boxes, redecorating the theatre, and replacing the old gallery benches with seats. He also improved the heating and ventilation systems, making it "possible for any invalid to safely enjoy the attractions of the stage."[13]

Throughout the 1890s and into the new century, the opera house offered much the same theatrical fare as during its first decade. Colorado Springs became a fixture on the Silver Circuit, so that companies usually started their Colorado tours there after performing for a week in Denver. Meanwhile Nye continued his practice of scheduling companies independently, especially reliable favorites like minstrel shows and comedy troupes. Concerts continued to be popular, with John Philip Sousa bringing his bands to town on several occasions. Shakespeare was also a surprisingly durable attraction, and audiences were privileged to see such star performers as Wilson Barrett in *Hamlet*, Helena Modjeska in *Henry VIII* and *As You Like It*, and Johnston Forbes-Robertson in *Hamlet*. As late as November 1913, Shakespeare great Robert Mantell appeared at the opera house in *Hamlet, Macbeth*, and *The Merchant of Venice*. The one constant in all these entertainments was a discriminating audience that demanded good value for its money. George M. Cohan, who performed there, said that "a cast had to work doubly hard to earn applause in Colorado Springs. The audiences will not settle for less than excellence."[14]

Along with Shakespeare, opera was considered the most sophisticated cultural event, and it was well represented in Colorado Springs. Probably the most notable production was *Madame Butterfly* in 1908, starring Dora de Fillippe from Milan, Puccini's own choice as Butterfly. The two performances were declared "the greatest production ever offered in Colorado Springs."[15] Other operas did not fare quite so well. The production of *Carmen* in 1910 featured Louise Le Baron, a diva notably taller than her leading man. "It is always distressing in real life to see a woman reach down to hug a man," wrote a reviewer, "and it is next to intolerable on the stage."[16] *Faust* was one of the more frequently performed operas, with variable success. In 1906, the English Grand Opera Company presented a thrilling production climaxed by a rain of fire descending on the stage and enveloping Mephistopheles. (The reviewer praised the pyrotechnics but criticized the audience for arriving late:

"They may have grown up in the east but have seemingly grown down in the west."[17]) By contrast, the last *Faust* performance at the opera house in 1914 by the New York Grand Opera Company was so spartan that the chorus numbers had to be sung by the principal singers.

Despite the continuity of Nye's administration and booking practices, changes were occurring that would affect the programs, audiences, and eventually the future of the opera house. The opening of the Coliseum Theatre in September 1894 did not offer serious competition to the entertainments of the opera house, but its showings of the biograph, triograph, mutoscope, variscope, and cameraphone forced Nye to offer these precursors of motion pictures, starting in 1896. Still, Nye always considered movies more of an oddity than a substantial entertainment, even as other movie houses were opened. After the turn of the century, he would often couple a movie with vaudeville, another opera house innovation starting in 1904. In 1910, his decision to present a film of the recent Jim Jeffries–Jack Johnson prizefight roused objections by local ministers. In a letter to the newspaper, Nye assured readers that he had seen the film in Denver, "at which there were as many ladies as men in the audience," and he had found nothing indecorous. He continued:

> *In the 30 years I have been manager of the Opera House, I have always endeavored to give the public only clean and decent attractions. A year ago I canceled "Three Weeks" because of its immoral theme. If I saw anything at all objectionable in the Jeffries–Johnson pictures, or if there were any sane reason why these pictures should not be shown at the Opera House, I would not play them.[18]*

Nye's reasoning prevailed, and the film was shown four times. In general, Nye remained faithful to the vision of the opera house founders, offering quality entertainment without resorting to the prizefights and circuses that became common at other Colorado theatres.

As motion pictures were on the rise, the old star system was in decline, and Nye responded by booking stock companies for extended periods starting in 1905. The Spooner–Wallock Stock Company enjoyed the longest consecutive run in Colorado Springs history up to that time, from June 21 to September 11, 1909, a record broken the following year by the Lorch Company. Nye usually engaged a company for a ninety-day summer season, with a new show opening each Monday night, and continued this practice each season till the end of his career.

Except for the proliferation of movie houses (four by 1912), the opera house had enjoyed little competition in offering first-class shows, but this favorable situation ended with the opening of the Burns Theatre in May 1912. With his own "Theatre Beautiful" and stock company, James Burns successfully attracted the same audiences that had patronized the opera house for years. The resignation of Simeon Nye as theatre manager on December 2, 1914, and his death three months later further weakened the status and viability of the opera house. It continued to operate for four more years, but in 1918 it was converted to a full-time movie theatre. Ten years later it was remodeled by its owner, Cyrus Ferguson, into the Ferguson Office Building, and it later operated as a Woolworth's store for forty years. Today the building houses several small bars and nightclubs. Traces of the original structure can be seen in the columns that supported the balcony and in remnants of the marble floor entry.

Burns Theatre

OPENED: MAY 8, 1912

CONVERTED TO A MOVIE THEATRE:

FEBRUARY 1928

CLOSED: OCTOBER 31, 1972

DEMOLISHED: MAY 1973

The story goes that the most beautiful theatre in Colorado Springs history originated in a snub. James F. "Jimmie" Burns, a one-time plumber who had made his fortune with the Portland Gold Mine at Cripple Creek, was refused his request to rent the Colorado Springs Opera House for a party. A tough but generous Scotch-Irishman from Maine, Burns took a dim view of Colorado Springs high society. In the words of historian Marshall Sprague, "He felt that he had seen much more of the world than most of these aristocrats and that it took more brains to repair a toilet than to talk bad French or race a gig along Cascade Avenue."[19] He did not respond impetuously to the perceived rebuff, but contemplated the building of a new theatre that would eclipse the opera house in grandeur and fill what he felt was a void in the cultural life of Colorado Springs.

Burns began in 1908 by purchasing property at 21 East Pikes Peak Avenue. He then

James Ferguson (Jimmie) Burns (1853-1917) struck it rich in Cripple Creek and built Colorado Springs its most beautiful theatre in 1912.
PHOTO COURTESY ANN AND TOM NAUGHTON

commissioned the local architectural firm of Douglas and Hetherington to design the theatre, and in 1910 he awarded the construction contract to James Stewart and Company, which had just completed the Exchange National Bank Building next door. The total construction cost would reach $350,000, over four times the cost of the opera house around the corner, partly because the Burns was built on such a grand scale. The auditorium could seat 1,400 people on three different levels—parquet, balcony, and gallery, plus six boxes (three on either side of the stage) in both the parquet and balcony. Yet despite its size, almost twice that of the Colorado Springs Opera House, patrons sat no farther than 90 feet from the stage and had an unobstructed view of its proceedings. The stage itself was 45 feet in depth and 65 feet wide, with a proscenium 65 feet high. Not only could the stage capacity accommodate spectacular productions, but its floor construction—four-inch lengths of 2-by-4s stood on end in a concrete base—gave it unusual strength and prevented splintering when heavy scenery or trunks were transported on its surface.

The entire theatre reflected both a love of opulence and attention to detail. The imposing facade was done in white glazed terra cotta in a renaissance style, and the carvings adorning the front were executed with particular artistry. One entered the theatre through a lobby

Façade of the Burns Theatre (undated, but taken a few years after the opening in 1912).

featuring floors, walls, banisters, and four huge pillars covered with polished Italian marble or, in some cases, painted plaster. (A pair of cupids that graced the lobby entrance can still be seen at Giuseppe's Depot Restaurant in Colorado Springs.) Two grand staircases ascended to the second floor, and elegant foyers extended the length of both the parquet and balcony. Inside the auditorium, the seats were upholstered in olive green velvet trimmed with beautiful wood. Enormous, blood-red draperies served as a stage

Detail of the glazed terra cotta façade of the Burns Theatre (date unknown).
PHOTO BY MYRON WOOD, (C) PIKES PEAK LIBRARY DISTRICT

The elegant lobby of the Burns Theatre, c. 1912. The grand staircase ascended to the balcony.
COLORADO SPRINGS PIONEERS MUSEUM

curtain. Overhead, gargoyles arched across the front of the proscenium, and murals done in oils were painted on the ceiling. Even the lavatories had marble basins and urinals as well as sparkling brass fixtures. With good reason, the Burns was always known as "The Theatre Beautiful."

Two features of the Burns were especially noteworthy and valuable. From the time of its opening, it was thought to have some of the best acoustics of any theatre in the country, and drawings of its design were later studied by experts in New York. The auditorium was extremely well insulated from noise because of its isolation from the street and its massive masonry construction. It also had the advantages of a high ceiling, balconies that did not extend too far over the floors below, and proximity of the audience to the stage. According to an engineering report published in 1973, sound was uniformly distributed and dead spots eliminated "by the use of precisely placed, correctly shaped reflective surfaces constructed of very heavy plaster and concrete attached to and supported by a superstructure so over engineered and over-constructed by today's standards that it approaches fantasy." The report concluded that the near-perfect acoustics "would be difficult, if not impossible, to achieve with today's construction techniques and funding restrictions."[20] When the well-known baritone, Chester Ludgin, visited Colorado Springs in October 1972 to help save the Burns from demolition, he tested the acoustics and stated, "They are among the best I have ever heard" and that natural acoustics so unusually good could not be duplicated.[21] The set designer from La Scala Opera House in Milan also praised the theatre's "warm, rich atmosphere for the performing arts" and thought it "reminiscent of the grand theatres of Europe."[22]

The Burns also had excellent sightlines, and the action on stage was clearly visible from any seat—a feature made possible by its unusual and graceful "hanging balconies," which were unsupported by columns. The balcony and gallery were attached to the outside walls of the auditorium by means of a "massive and complex" support system, a unique design at the time.[23] (In modern newspaper accounts of the Burns, it is amusing how often reporters have praised these suspended balconies, then illustrated them with photographs of the old opera house, with its traditional supporting pillars.) Local residents were hesitant to trust the safety of these seemingly unsupported balconies, so 2,200 sandbags, 100 pounds each, had to be placed in individual seats to prove the whole structure would not collapse. All fears were alleviated by opening night, when the balconies were filled with patrons who were "simply delighted with the position, for the ventilation is perfect, [and] the line of vision admirable."[24] The sightlines were also enhanced by the unusually steep floor of the auditorium, which made the view from the gallery

The auditorium of the Burns Theatre under construction, September 23, 1911. Hundred-pound sandbags were placed throughout the upper levels to prove that the hanging balconies, which were unsupported by columns, would not collapse when occupied by theatregoers.

PHOTO COURTESY DENVER PUBLIC LIBRARY, WESTERN HISTORY COLLECTION, X-14863

especially breathtaking, "like being on the side of a mountain, staring almost straight down." [25]

The many innovative and decorous features of the Burns contributed to a splendid opening night on May 8, 1912. Burns had thought of everything, including a system of managing the arrival and departure of carriages and automobiles to ease congestion at the theatre's entrance. "The flower of Colorado Springs society" turned out in all its glory, and "In honor of the occasion the display of handsome costly gowns lavishly garnitured with rare heirloom laces and jewels was an exceedingly notable one." [26] All seats were sold, plus fifty standing-room tickets, and hundreds of people were turned away for the "Grand Spring Musical Festival" provided by the sixty-member Russian Symphony Orchestra and its conductor, Modest Altschuler. The long program consisted of Wagner's Overture to *Tannhauser*, arias from well-known operas, dances by the Russian ballerina Lydia Lopoukowa, a medley of American patriotic songs sung by opera stars Henri La Bonte and Vera Curtis, and, in conclusion,

Tchaikovsky's *1812 Overture*, then as now a Colorado Springs favorite. An encore of "Dixie" drew thunderous applause, and both "Columbia, the Gem of the Ocean" and "The Star Spangled Banner" brought the audience to its feet. In the course of the evening, Chester Alan Arthur II, son of former president Chester A. Arthur, rose from his box and addressed James Burns, "to voice the general public sentiment of gratitude to you, which the opening of this beautiful theater inspires…. May it long continue to shelter all that is best in art and music, and remain as a monument to the generosity and enterprise of its founder, James F. Burns."[27] Burns responded by pledging that his theatre would continue to be a mecca of Colorado Springs culture.

For the next few years, Burns kept that pledge by presenting the same type of high-class entertainments that had distinguished the Colorado Springs Opera House. Starting in June 1912, he featured a summer stock company that performed a new play each week, plus matinees on Tuesdays and Saturdays, for twenty-eight weeks. Concerts and lectures were occasionally interspersed, as well as George M. Cohan's *Forty-Five Minutes from Broadway* on July 29, 1912, which drew 10,000 people during its one-week engagement. However, Burns lost

The splendid auditorium of the Burns Theatre, c. 1912, with seating capacity of 1,400.

COURTESY, PIKES PEAK LIBRARY DISTRICT

money when he paid a large guarantee to the Chicago Grand Opera Company for its performance of *The Secret of Suzanne* on October 24, 1912. The local newspaper commented that guarantees of this sort were risky, and that Simeon Nye at the opera house "has long declared that he would not guarantee the Passion Play with the original cast."[28]

Such miscalculations were rare, and the Burns's second year was even more profitable. Seven concerts, a dance recital, and a lecture preceded the fourteen-week appearance of the summer stock company starting on June 9, 1913. "It is not out of place to remark on the general excellence of the company, upon the particular happy selection of plays that have been given, and upon the artistic, and even lavish staging that has been produced," a reviewer wrote. "Cities many times the size of Colorado Springs have stock companies in no way comparable with the Burns players."[29] A successful pattern had been established, and the following year the summer stock company drew over 10,000 people in one week for *Stop Thief*, part of its twelve-week repertory. Other notables who appeared at the Burns in 1914 included the pianist Ignace Paderewski, Helen Keller, and Harry Lauder.

Between 1914 and 1920, events conspired to change the repertory of the Burns. In 1912, Burns had declined the opportunity to purchase the National Theater Owners Association franchise from Simeon Nye, who sold it instead to the Colorado Springs Opera House Company. Without this franchise, Burns could book only the occasional touring company traveling through Colorado. To compensate and to keep his theatre open, he continued to rely on stock companies and, by 1915, on both vaudeville and motion pictures. Vaudeville made its debut on April 11, 1915, and the following season the Burns was advertising "the only High-class vaudeville circuit."[30] Meanwhile, the first movie projector was installed in 1915, with movies being shown two nights a week.

Jimmie Burns died in 1917 and his son-in-law, William Nicholson, became owner and manager. Nicholson continued Burns's booking practices. A typical weekly program of 1920 featured Pentages Vaudeville on Monday and Tuesday nights, a movie or road show on Wednesday and Thursday, and Junior Orpheum Vaudeville on Friday and Saturday. Like the Colorado Springs Opera House, the Burns also sometimes served as a civic auditorium, hosting high-school graduations as well as, on May 27, 1918, "300 Girl Scouts of Colorado Springs" in *Converting Mrs. Noshuns*, "With Patriotic Curtain Raiser and Final Tableau."[31]

While yielding gradually to popular tastes, the Burns did not forsake high-class productions completely. Walter Hampden, the renowned Shakespearean actor, starred in *Othello* on March 20, 1922, playing the title role "with cyclonic power and marvelous impressiveness," which unfortunately underscored the weakness of his supporting cast.[32] Two months later, John Drew appeared in Maugham's recent play, *The Circle*, which ends with the married heroine, Elizabeth Champion-Cheney, unexpectedly running off with another man. The local reviewer found the play unsettling, for "a phase of life is pictured as it is and not as people like to think of it. Others have done it, of course, but not so brutally."[33] Both productions were enthusiastically applauded, no small accomplishment when compared with the response of a more typical Burns audience in 1922 to Ethel Barrymore in *Declasse*:

> *Possibly Miss Barrymore has found audiences colder than that at the Burns last evening, but surely not often. Late, as usual, in arriving, people settled down finally in the attitude, "Well, we're ready; go ahead, and arouse us, if you can." Nor thruout the evening was there anything but a superficial demonstrativeness.* [34]

Concerts were still an occasional draw, especially with performers like the Austrian pianist Arthur Schnabel, who played at the Burns on February 7, 1923. He was followed one week later by the composer and pianist Sergei Rachmaninoff, the "Russian musical colossus," who played Beethoven's *Appassionata* sonata. The local paper exulted, "We were listening to a master musician reproducing most eloquently the thought of a kindred spirit."[35] Rosa Ponselle, "without question the first dramatic soprano of the land,"[36] performed at the Burns in 1922 and again in 1926. In her first appearance, she "accomplished what no other singer has been able to do" when she sang Verdi's "Pace, pace mio Dio" from *La Forza del Destino* and "roused our somewhat undemonstrative audience into a state of enthusiasm which in itself proved thrilling."[37]

Such memorable evenings became more and more exceptional, and by 1926, the Burns was showing films six days a week. The following year Nicholson completely remodeled the theatre at a cost of $80,000, added a modern projection booth, and installed a $30,000, 500-pipe Wurlitzer organ. (The organ is still played at the City Auditorium during summer concerts.) But it soon became clear that the Burns could no longer operate as an independent movie theatre, since movie chains were being formed across the country to distribute films more efficiently and profitably. In February 1928, the theatre was leased to Paramount Publix under a contract that excluded its showing of legitimate drama. Thus ended the glory days of the "Theatre Beautiful" after only sixteen years.

The Burns, however, survived another forty-five years with at least some of its dignity and history intact. In 1933 the lease was taken over by Westland Theatre Corporation, which renamed the building the Chief Theatre, added an unsightly marquee above the entrance, and showed primarily films but also occasional road shows as late as 1951. The beginning of the end came in 1965 when Mrs. Will Nicholson, the daughter of James Burns, leased the theatre to the Exchange National Bank with the option that, under certain circumstances, the building could be demolished. Despite the efforts of a "Save the Burns" movement, which included having the Burns entered in the National Registry of Historic Places on March 6, 1973, the Colorado Springs City Council was not persuaded that the theatre fit into its plans to build a downtown mall and convention center, which later became the Pikes Peak Center. According to DeRos Hogue, secretary of the Landmarks Preservation Council of the Pikes Peak Region and a leading proponent of the Burns preservation, "when the chips were down, the public would not come forward to make its feelings known and the City Council was hesitant to act in opposition to the Bank's plans."[38] Instead, to make way for a parking lot, the theatre was closed for the last time on October 31, 1972, and demolished in May 1973, marking the end of a structure described by Marshall Sprague as the handsomest building in town and remembered by many as a "landmark jewel."[39]

PUEBLO

Pueblo Grand Opera House

OPENED: OCTOBER 9, 1890

DESTROYED BY FIRE: MARCH 1, 1922

Unlike the Colorado Springs Opera House and Burns Theatre, which were conceived and financed by a few individuals, the Pueblo Grand Opera House was built by public subscription as a mark of civic pride and "substantial evidence of the metropolitan tendencies"[40] of the young city. Founded on July 1, 1860, Pueblo enjoyed a population and economic boom with the arrival of the Denver & Rio Grande Railroad in 1872; the Atchison, Topeka & Santa Fe Railroad in 1876; and the start of the Colorado Coal & Iron Company in 1881. By the early 1880s, Pueblo had developed a vibrant economy based on its steel mill and smelting as well as banking and farming, and was known as "the Pittsburgh of the West." Its population of 24,558 in 1890 was second only to Denver's. But its leaders envisioned something more, "a great manufacturing city whose wealth and influence will be second to none in the magnificent empire of the west,"[41] and they looked for ways to bolster its reputation both economically and culturally.

Pueblo had already housed at least twenty-nine different theatres or performance halls by 1888. But when the DeRemer Opera House, a converted roller-skating rink, was damaged by fire on May 1 of that year, city leaders formed the Pueblo Grand Opera House Association and contributed $115,000 (including the site, valued at $40,000), and further proposed to raise an additional $135,000 by public subscription in exchange for shares of stock. A local judge declared in a speech that "an opera house was an indication of advanced civilization and refinement on the part of the people in whose city it was erected, that Pueblo must have an opera house at once and that she ought to get one commensurate with her late marvellous successes." He concluded that this structure would help to "inaugurate a substantial boom of unprecedented proportions."[42] Such notions were widely shared at the time. When Horace Tabor visited Pueblo a few days later, he told a group of citizens,

. . . the proposed Grand opera house would be a success[,] that when the Tabor Grand was built Denver was not as large as Pueblo is now, and people laughed at the idea of building an opera house of such magnificent proportions, but that the laugh was soon on the other side, and that the erection of that opera house has long been conceded to have been the first great step in making Denver a metropolitan city, and calling the attention of outsiders to its location and advantages.[43]

The actions of Pueblo's civic leaders matched their aspirations when, in 1888, they commissioned the nationally known firm of Adler and Sullivan from Chicago to design a palatial opera house. By the time Louis H. Sullivan visited Pueblo on June 30, 1888, plans for the new opera house were well underway. Similar to the Tabor Grand, the four-story building would be part of an "opera house block" with business offices flanking the opera house on either side, principally the First National Bank on the southeast corner of the ground floor. It would occupy a space 120 by 190 feet on the northwest corner of Fourth and Main Streets (now occupied by the Colorado Building), a site donated by John Albert Thatcher, Mahlon D. Thatcher, and Oliver H. P. Baxter. Building costs were estimated at $368,000, a figure that rose to an actual cost of about $500,000. After some delay in the firm's final plans, construction began on February 5, 1889, and proceeded with little deviation from the original design under the supervision of Henry W. French, with additional visits to the site by both Sullivan and his partner, Dankmar Adler.

Historians have speculated that Frank Lloyd Wright, then an aspiring architect with Adler and Sullivan, may actually deserve more credit than Sullivan for the design of the opera house. This suggestion seems unlikely, however, given the similarities between the building and the Chicago Auditorium that Adler and Sullivan were also constructing at the time, the publicity for which helped to win them the Pueblo contract. For example, the striking masonry exterior, cut into large rectangular blocks of Manitou red sandstone, was similar to that used in the Auditorium. So was the intricate, low-relief carving, "designed to suggest the peculiar thorny effects of Colorado cacti,"[44] although Wright may have assisted with such decorative details. Sullivan's trademark, however, was the Italian-style tower directly above the entrance to the opera house, rising 131 feet above the sidewalk and accessible by elevator. As Sullivan explained, "It was natural that there should be a tower to mark from a distance the location of the building, and no more

proper place could be found for it than over the entrance to the theater."[45] Directly behind the tower, Sullivan added a rooftop summer garden featuring a ballroom surrounded by windows and flowering plants.
Despite the roof garden's attractiveness to Pueblo society as a favorite
partying place, its construction of wood rather than stone would be the
downfall of the opera house just thirty-two years later.

The main entrance to the theatre on the Main Street side was
grand indeed. One walked under an archway that formed part of a
square facade projecting slightly from the building, with detailed
stonework and medallion carvings of Verdi and Shakespeare, both of
whom were performed at the opera house. Crossing through an arcade
and a tiled vestibule, which contained the box office and stairways to
upper levels of the theatre, the playgoer entered the auditorium through
a large doorway leading to a series of rounded arches. Inside, one's attention was immediately drawn to two large barrel vaults, the first projecting from the proscenium, the other at right angles to it and forming a

Exterior of the Pueblo Grand Opera House (date unknown). Smoke appears to
be coming from the roof, an unfortunate harbinger of the fire that would destroy
the opera house thirty-two years after its opening, in 1922.
PHOTOGRAPH COURTESY PUEBLO CITY–COUNTY LIBRARY DISTRICT

The main entrance of the Pueblo Grand Opera House (date unknown). Note the medallion portraits of Verdi (on the left) and Shakespeare.
PHOTOGRAPH COURTESY PUEBLO CITY-COUNTY LIBRARY DISTRICT, SUHAY COLLECTION

paneled ceiling with rosettes in each panel. The expansive interior, measuring 78 feet in width and 85 feet from the curtain to the doors, allowed for a seating capacity of 1,100, nearly that of the Tabor Grand in Denver and one of the largest in Colorado.

Patrons were seated on one of three levels: a combination parquet and slightly raised parquet circle, separated by a wire railing, with four open proscenium boxes on either side of the stage; a sweeping balcony supported by a series of arches (and thus no pillars to obstruct a view of the stage); and a gallery running straight across the rear of the auditorium. The primary color of the interior was salmon, with a contrasting ceiling in gray blue, and gold and ivory covering the proscenium, side arches, and the fronts of the balcony and gallery. Although there was no chandelier, 500 electric lights embedded in the ornamentation gave the theatre "a brilliantly beautiful and warm effect."[46] One distinguished visitor on opening night, William Guggenheim from Philadelphia, thought the opera house was "not as fine as Denver's but nevertheless quite fancy."[47]

View of the stage and auditorium, Pueblo Grand Opera House, October 10, 1890.
AUTHORS' COLLECTION

Side view of the auditorium, Pueblo Grand Opera House, October 10, 1890. From this position one can see the unusual barrel vault of the paneled ceiling, with rosettes in each panel.
AUTHORS' COLLECTION

The only known photograph of the stage and drop curtain of the Pueblo Grand Opera House, apparently based on the setting of Tennyson's poem, "The Brook" (date unknown).
REPRINTED FROM THE BOOK OF THE PLAY/GRAND OPERA HOUSE, PUEBLO. DENVER PUBLIC LIBRARY, WESTERN HISTORY COLLECTION

The stage, 90 feet wide and 75 feet high, 40 feet in depth, with an opening 32 feet in width and 30 feet high in the center of the proscenium, was immediately recognized as "one of the finest and best equipped in the United States."[48] Among other features, it had twenty trapdoors and other openings in the stage floor; a large collection of new scenery, which could be manipulated from the loft above the stage rather than from the sides; and seven hundred red, white, and green electric lights. Perhaps most striking were the two splendid drop curtains. One was a painted landscape of hills, trees, and "chattering brook" (apparently taken from the setting of Tennyson's poem "The Brook");

The only known photograph of the auditorium, Pueblo Grand Opera House (date unknown).

the other was a pink satin curtain appliquéd with lyres and dotted with rhinestones—and both looked marvelous in the well-lit auditorium. An automatic sprinkler system for the stage was planned but never installed.

The original contract had called for the opera house to be completed in fourteen months, but the opening night was delayed till October 9, 1890. Considering the many Chicago connections in the design and outfitting of the theatre, it was appropriate that the first program was presented by the 100-member Duff Opera Company of Chicago in Gilbert and Sullivan's *Iolanthe*. "No such enthusiastic and brilliant audience was ever assembled in Pueblo as that at the Grand Opera house to-night,"[49] a local reviewer wrote, as patrons willingly paid the advertised ticket prices—$3.00 for the parquet, parquet circle, and two front rows of the balcony; $2.50 for the balcony (the only part of the theatre with vacant seats at the premiere); $1.00 for the gallery; and $100 or $50 for a box at all four of the Duff performances. The powerful orchestra and chorus did justice to the fine acoustics and excellent sightlines of the theatre, and performances by Thigby Bell as the Lord High Chancellor and Louise Beaudet as Iolanthe were especially noteworthy. In the course of the evening, Oliver H. P. Baxter, who had brought electric lighting and trolleys to Pueblo in addition to being the chief supporter of the opera house, was recognized with the presentation of a large basket of Colorado wildflowers and the proclamation that "the children of generations to come would rise from their seats in that splendid opera house to call Mr. Baxter blessed."[50] Later in the week, the Duff Company continued its engagement in *The Pirates of Penzance, Patience*, and *The Mikado*, as the "magnificent Palace of Amusement" made its debut in fine style.

Shortly after the opening on November 21, 1890, Simeon Nye, manager of the Colorado Springs Opera House, succeeded Nick Loritz as manager of the Pueblo Grand. Meanwhile, Peter McCourt quickly signed up the theatre (at a cost of $10,000) as a new stop on the Silver Circuit. However, few visiting companies utilized the resources of the theatre as fully as the Duff Company had, and Pueblo itself had little local drama to offer. The growing popularity of movie houses and vaudeville also encroached on the numbers of people attending the theatre. To compete, the opera house installed its own projector and throughout much of its existence was used as a movie theatre. Finally, only three years after the theatre opened, the stock market panic of 1893 slowed investment and expansion in the West, thwarting Pueblo's dream of becoming a major city in the region, that distinction being held by Denver to the north and Santa Fe (the main railroad hub) to the south.

Despite these disappointments, the Pueblo Grand hosted many distinguished performances during its all-too-brief lifetime. Helena Modjeska transported her company, and a sixty-foot railway car full of scenery, to the opera house for a performance of *Henry VIII* on March 14, 1893. Modjeska displayed "noble womanliness" as Katherine, Otis Skinner was "full of the fire and arrogance" of King Henry, and the play was beautifully staged with historically appropriate costumes and settings. The entire company was strong, "without that discrepancy in capacity which is sometimes characteristic of stars who wish to shine in all their radiance, made more conspicuous by the mediocre acting of others around them."[51]

Another notable Shakespearean, Robert Mantell, also brought a capable supporting cast for his performance of *Macbeth* on January 16,

1912. The audience especially appreciated the "distinctness of enuncia-tion that made it possible for the audience to hear the words of the great Shakespeare, as well as to behold the talent of the justly reknowned *[sic]* dramatic star."[52] Mantell also took the opportunity the day before to marry Genevieve Hamper, a member of his company, and host a wed-ding supper served on the opera house stage. He returned the follow-ing year to present *Hamlet, The Merchant of Venice*, and *King Lear*.

As with other opera houses on the Silver Circuit, the secret of suc-cess in Pueblo was variety. The fall of 1893 saw Mrs. John Drew appear as Mrs. Malaprop in Sheridan's *The Rivals* on August 29, a fine perform-ance that nevertheless drew only a fair house. One reviewer missed her famous co-stars (Joseph Jefferson, W. J. Florence, and John Gilbert) in this play, so that "a feeling almost of sadness comes over one who has seen the full constellation."[53] Audiences were no more enthusiastic about two "stereopticon views" (magic lantern shows), *Urania* and *A Trip to the Moon*, on September 5. However, when Katie Emmett appeared on September 26 in *Killarney*, she drew the largest audiences in months at both the Pueblo and Colorado Springs theatres. Cleveland's Minstrels on October 24 performed to an equally crowded house.

Opera itself was not a frequent visitor to Pueblo, despite the excel-lent stage facilities. However, in the space of two days, on September 29-30, 1899, Lambardi's Italian Grand Opera Company staged *Carmen, Norma*, and *Il Travatore*. While fashionable audiences were appreciative of the performances, a reviewer pointed out the hazards of a traveling company presenting grand opera:

> *The indifference exhibited by the orchestra might be attributed to the fact that they are handicapped by the absence of a second violin, oboe, bassoon and tympanies, to say nothing of a second horn and extra first violin. The director is forced to help out the string section with the piano. There is no director living who can direct a work as pre-tentious as "Carmen" and play piano at the same time, doing jus-tice to both.*[54]

Other celebrities who appeared at the opera house included Sarah Bernhardt, the Russian dancer Pavlova, and two U.S. presidents, Theodore Roosevelt and William Howard Taft.

The end of the Pueblo Grand came suddenly. Early in the morn-ing of March 1, 1922, a fire started in the roof garden, which had been used the prior evening for the annual ball of the Pueblo Grocers' Association. It was never known what started the blaze, but possibly a

The Pueblo Grand Opera House was destroyed March 1, 1922, by a fire that started in the roof garden (date unknown). The intense cold caused water from the fire hoses to freeze on the building.
PHOTOGRAPH COURTESY PUEBLO CITY–COUNTY LIBRARY DISTRICT

discarded cigarette ignited wrapping paper that covered the floor—the remains of sacks of groceries awarded, quite appropriately, as prizes for good dancing. Only thirty-five minutes after the fire was discovered, the main roof collapsed, and within an hour the entire opera house block was destroyed. Firefighters fought the blaze as well as strong winds and bitterly cold temperatures estimated at thirteen below zero, but their efforts were futile. The water from the fire hoses froze on the charred shell of the building, leaving an ice sculpture, magnificent in its own way, that lasted for several days.

Thus ended one of the largest and most ornate theatres in Colorado's history, a monument to the vision and ambition of Pueblo's first citizens. Still recovering from the disastrous flood of the Arkansas River in June 1921, which had inundated the opera house and required three months of pumping to remove, the city could not afford a rebuilding effort. None of the theatre survives, although the nearby post office and Thatcher Building, constructed when the opera house still stood, attempted to harmonize with their distinguished neighbor by incorporating such features as the ground-story arches, tiled entryways, and some of the ornamentation. By these means, the long-absent theatre still casts a ghostly shadow over its locale. Also the handsome and well-presered Union Depot, built in 1889, displays the same type of Manitou red sandstone used in the Pueblo Grand.

CHAPTER SIX

REPRESENTATIVE THEATRES OF COLORADO

In addition to the major theatres discussed elsewhere, Colorado had a number of other significant opera houses built before the turn of the century. One of these, the McClellan Opera House in Georgetown, was the first so-called opera house in the territory of Colorado. Three other theatres—the Jaffa Opera House in Trinidad, the Salida Opera House, and the Park Opera House in Grand Junction—were stops along the famous and far-flung Silver Circuit. The fifth theatre, the Wright Opera House in Ouray, is remarkable for its longevity in a relatively remote location. These theatres' architectural splendor and contribution to the cultural and social life of their communities make them worthy of remembrance.

GEORGETOWN
McClellan Opera House

OPENED: JULY 2, 1869

DESTROYED BY FIRE: JANUARY 10, 1892

The small, charming community of Georgetown might seem an unlikely spot for the first opera house in Colorado, until we recall that in 1875, it was the third largest town in the state, next only to Denver and Central City. George Griffith first discovered gold in the region in August 1859, but it was the silver strikes in 1864, and especially the opening of the Anglo-Saxon Mine in 1867 that assayed up to $23,000 a ton, that established Georgetown

Artist's reconstruction of the McClellan Opera House in Georgetown (date unknown).

Drop curtain, McClellan Opera House (date unknown).
PHOTO COURTESY DENVER PUBLIC LIBRARY, WESTERN HISTORY COLLECTION, F-20931

as the "Silver Queen," the greatest silver-mining town in the world. Erskine McClellan arrived in Clear Creek County by at least 1864 and was financially successful as both a miner and smelter. Although Georgetown's population in 1869 was only 800 or so, McClellan determined that, as one of the town's leading citizens, he should erect a public assembly and performance hall that would also provide space for his wife's furniture store.

Construction of the two-story frame building began in February 1869 at the intersection of Taos and Alpine (now Sixth) Streets. No photograph of the complete structure has ever been found, but from newspaper accounts, the building appears to have been 25 by 57 ½ feet, with the theatre on the upper floor and the furniture store below, and the entrance to the theatre on the Taos Street side. Seating capacity must have been quite limited at first, perhaps about 200 removable seats, since the theatre's remodeling in 1873 *increased* capacity to over three hundred. The stage was approximately 30 feet wide and 50 feet deep. We do not even know what performance inaugurated the opera house on July 2, 1869, the local newspaper stating only, "The Concert Hall and Dance-House ... opened in a blaze of glory last night. It is as near as we come to having a theatre in Georgetown."[1]

Georgetown probably faced more inherent disadvantages than any other important theatre town in the state, chief among them being its inaccessibility. Located in the mountains at an altitude of 8,640 feet, it was difficult and often hazardous to reach by wagon or coach. Even with the arrival of the Colorado Central Railroad in August 1877, the trip was slow, expensive, and inconvenient, since Georgetown was literally the end of the line: the train either had to return to Denver or attempt to cross the mountain passes. The route was not without its dangers, as when McMahon's Circus tried to reach Georgetown in August 1891:

> *McMahon's big elephants derailed the train last Monday while coming up to Georgetown. They were too top-heavy for the narrow-gauge track, and in swinging around a curve at Fall River, the elephants were lurched to one side and upset the cars. . . . One of [the circus hands] was caught under a car, and one of the elephants brought into service to release him. He lifted the car as easily as a man would a stick of wood.* [2]

Also, Georgetown was largely dependent on Denver for its theatrical entertainment, and when business was poor in Denver, surrounding mining towns like Georgetown suffered as well. Finally, the people of Georgetown were usually happy with amateur dramatic groups and never felt compelled to erect a more ostentatious theatre to attract famous professional actors or touring companies. In 1881 the local newspaper editor urged his readers to invest $25,000 in a new opera house: "The people of Central [City], a smaller place than Georgetown, clubbed together a few years ago and built a nice, cosy opera house which is a credit to the town, and we are very loathe to admit that the people of our neighboring city have more enterprise than those of our own."[3] But such appeals to civic pride went for naught.

Despite these obstacles, the McClellan hosted a steady and varied stream of entertainers in its early days, including John Kelly ("The Ole Bull of the West") with his partner, Master Willie, an Indian contortionist; the Alfred E. Mathews Panorama of Rocky Mountain Views; the Shoo Fly Minstrels; Satsuma's Royal Japanese Troupe; and most remarkably, the Fanny B. Price Company for a period of six weeks in August 1872. Referring to the latter group, the *Colorado Miner* judged that "for the first time in our history, the theatre-going portion of our 'Silver-Queen,' [is] now being entertained by a *first-class* company,"[4] appearing in such plays as *Pauline* and *Camille*. The excitement was considerably augmented one Saturday night during the Price Company's stay when *as the play in McClellan's Hall was progressing, a lamp fell down and spreading [sic] fire and consternation through the hall. Some jumped out of the windows, others rushed for the doors, one of the lady actresses fainted and fell upon the stage. There was a complete panic, but things were righted up before much harm was done, and the play was finished.[5]*

At times when there were no performances booked, the opera house was also used as a skating rink.

When William H. Cushman, a banker and financier, erected a three-story building diagonally across the street from the McClellan and installed a comfortable theatre on the third floor, the new Cushman Opera House quickly became Georgetown's favorite performance hall, opening on Christmas Day 1875. But the Cushman was destined to remain in operation only four years, being doomed by its poor construction and finally condemned for public use in January 1880. Meanwhile, McClellan had overhauled his theatre in 1879, putting in a new floor, leveling the stage, removing the private boxes, and repainting the interior, "so that now it will compare favorably with any house in the State."[6]

After the remodeling, Georgetown entered the period of its greatest theatrical renown, with such stars as Kate Claxton appearing in *The Two Orphans* and *Frou Frou* in June 1879 and again in April 1881; Thomas W. Keene and Company performing in *Richard III*, *The Merchant of Venice*, and *Richelieu* in June 1881; and the trage-dienne Madame Janauschek starring in *Mother and Son* in May 1882. Two years earlier, on January 9, 1880, Janauschek had been the last per-former to appear at Cushman's, as Mary, Queen of Scots; rumor had it that the excitement of the audience had put such a strain on the supporting timbers that the

Renowned Czech actress Fanny Janauschek (1830-1904) in 1883, shortly after her appearance in Georgetown at the Cushman Opera House.
UNIVERSITY OF WASHINGTON LIBRARIES, SPECIAL COLLECTIONS, UW25108Z

building never recovered. She did not have the same effect at the McClellan, according to a reviewer, the result of both a less interesting drama and that "the play was pruned down, a thing that many first-class companies indulge in when playing in the smaller towns."[7]

The winter weather often had an unexpected role to play in the Georgetown theatre. In May 1880, the Pinafore Company was delayed by soft snow on the road from Leadville and arrived in Georgetown one day late. The newspaper noted, "Their baggage did not get through on time and consequently they were compelled to appear without costume, but notwithstanding that fact they give *[sic]* an excellent entertainment."[8] Sometimes even the audience was at risk. When the Miln Company performed *Macbeth* during a cold snap in December 1884, the theatre was so poorly heated that "a great many of the audience contracted severe colds from which they are still suffering. The management should appoint a stoker."[9] Rarely did the weather deter the hearty Georgetown residents, although it did prevail for a performance in January 1886 by the Langdon Company:

> *During the evening the windstorm raged with fury and the atmosphere within the hall was freezing cold. Although there were only about a dozen people in the audience in consequence of the weather, the company rendered the play in a first-class manner. The music and acting were both good. Immediately before appearing here they had been in a snow-bank in Nebraska for three day[s]. They evidently struck a very bad streak of luck.*[10]

As it happened, the cold weather that was so much a part of the McClellan's history also figured in its demise. At 10 o'clock in the morning on January 10, 1892, McClellan himself was under the building trying to thaw some frozen pipes with hot coals and irons. How the fire started, McClellan himself could not say; perhaps he accidentally ignited the wood shavings that served as insulation in the walls. The fire shot quickly to the top floor, and Mrs. McClellan had to be rescued from her living quarters by being carried through one of the upstairs windows. Any hope of saving the theatre was soon dashed when one of the fire hoses froze and could not be used for twenty minutes. The fire burned for four hours, and the opera house was a total loss, estimated at $10,000. It was never rebuilt, and today the lot is still vacant, marked only by a bronze plaque that commemorates this pioneer of Colorado's opera houses.

TRINIDAD

Jaffa Opera House

OPENED: OCTOBER 23, 1882

CONDEMNED: C. 1906

CURRENTLY AN APARTMENT COMPLEX

The most intriguingly named opera house in Colorado was built in the city of Trinidad, an intriguing name in itself and one whose origins are disputed. Possibly named for the Holy Trinity, Trinidad is located on the Purgatoire River, lying at the foot of Raton Pass just thirteen miles from the New Mexico border. It was first surveyed in 1861 and incorporated as a town in 1876. Trinidad originally prospered as a trading post on the Santa Fe Trail and as a commercial center for the surrounding cattle and sheep ranches. But coal made the town wealthy and gave it the nickname "Black Diamond Capital of Colorado." Not only did the coal lands extend over 600,000 acres, which were served by several mines in 1888, but the bituminous coal itself was considered the only coking coal (used for smelting) in the West. Where coal led, the railroad soon followed. Because of a dispute with the town, the Denver & Rio Grande Railroad originally went through El Moro, five miles distant from Trinidad, so travelers had to make the trip by hackney coach. By 1880, however, when the town's population had reached 2,226, both the Denver & Rio Grande and the Atchison, Topeka & Santa Fe Railroads stopped at Trinidad.

Trinidad was also the home of a relatively large Jewish population, as well as the oldest Colorado Jewish congregation in continuous existence (Congregation Aaron) aside from Denver. Two prominent members of that community, Sol and Henry Jaffa, had been employed by a mercantile firm in New Mexico and decided to open their own Trinidad store, called Jaffa Brothers General Merchandise, in 1871. They were joined two years later by their brother, Samuel. In a 1933 interview, Sol Jaffa recalled, "Business was very good then[,] merchants doing a large business with cattle and sheep men as far south as the Panhandle of Texas. Trinidad was the best trading place in this section of the country."[11] The Jaffas' store, which specialized in dry goods, was so successful that in 1878 they bought a building at the corner of West Main and

Commercial, still the most prominent intersection in Trinidad. *The Pueblo Chieftain* reported the following:

> *Jaffa Bros. have moved in the building formerly occupied by the Bank of Southern Colorado, and are now erecting a magnificent stone structure, the front columns of which will be each a single stone, twelve or fifteen feet high. In fact, no expense will be spared to make the building not only substantial, serviceable and beautiful, but really magnificent.*[12]

It is not known when the Jaffa Brothers decided to convert the second floor of this building to an opera house, or why. Newspaper accounts suggest they were responding to a demand in the Trinidad community for a cultural center and amusement place to match the prosperous town's business reputation. Construction was underway in 1882, and on June 17 of that year, the *Trinidad Daily News* reported that the drop curtain had been delivered, and "It is such an away up affair that it took two transfer wagons and four horses to haul it from the depot to the hall."[13] In early October, the opera house was lit for the first time and was immediately described as "the best in the state outside of Denver."[14]

The opening entertainment was provided by the Osborne Dramatic Company on October 23, 1882, although the doors were actually opened a few days earlier to admit the Las Animas County

Exterior of the Jaffa Opera House, Trinidad, 1888.

Democratic Convention. The editor of the *Trinidad Weekly News* "was only able to take a couple of peeps into the Opera House last night, but he saw that a well dressed, clean and well behaved audience had gone there to witness the opening entertainment. The plaudits which reached the sanctum three floors below indicated that the people were getting what they paid for."[15]

In his 1933 interview, Sol Jaffa barely mentioned the opera house and said only that "the second floor was used for traveling companies of Musicans [sic]."[16] He apparently intended it for modest productions by local acting companies and touring groups, and for concerts, balls, religious services, community meetings, and recitations. This preference may explain the small dimensions, with a stage only 30 feet wide and 24 feet deep, a proscenium opening 22 feet wide and 16 feet high, and a seating capacity of about 710. Glenn Aultman, whose family ran its photography studio from the same location on Main Street for all of the twentieth century, remembers that the stage "wasn't big enough for a real, big-city style play" and that productions "had to be greatly abbreviated when they played there."[17]

Throughout its early years, the Jaffa played host to a wide variety of performances, often before enthusiastic audiences. In what one reviewer called "the first genuine, good performance ever tendered to

Interior of the Jaffa Opera House, 1888. Seats on the main floor appear to be permanently installed rather than removable, as was usually the case with small-town theatres.

REPRINTED FROM TRINIDAD DIRECTORY (1888),
COURTESY COLORADO HISTORICAL SOCIETY

the people of Trinidad," the Frank Mordaunt Combination presented the popular play, *Old Shipmates*, on November 11, 1882. He elaborated, "The performance … fully demonstrates what effect a good play in a first-class house produces. The stage settings and scenery effects were shown to brilliant advantage, and were duly recognized by hearty applause."[18] When Jennie Woltz played in *The Daughter of the Regiment* on January 11, 1883, the *Trinidad Daily News* thought she "came out supreme. Not only was Miss Jennie's acting throughout the play superb, but the singing was more than heavenly, the best we have ever heard in Trinidad. . . . Each time she sung she was heartily encored, and to each encore she graciously responded by producing another beautiful song."[19] Two nights later, the Louie Lord Combination returned to Trinidad to perform in an unnamed farce before a mostly full house. The reviewer reflected:

> *The truth is, in a city no larger than Trinidad the company is always the most popular that makes the most fun, and it is strange that the show people do not find this out. People see enough of malice, suffering, slander and cruelty in their everyday experience in life. They do not care, night after night, to witness the portrayal of the scenes of the day, and pay for it in the bargain. . . . In short, we all want to laugh.*[20]

In August 1887, one of the Jaffa brothers arranged with Peter McCourt for their theatre to be included on the Silver Circuit, evidently from a desire to bring a higher class of entertainment to Trinidad. Instead of being limited to lesser names or local talents, patrons of the opera house could now enjoy such stars as Mademoiselle Rhea, who appeared in the French adaptation *Fairy Fingers* on April 30, 1888.

In 1895, the Jaffas sold their opera house block to move their mercantile business to another location in town. Touring companies continued to visit the Jaffa, as it was called until early in the new century when it was rechristened the Trinidad Opera House, the name that is still visible today above the former entrance. By 1906-7, however, the old theatre was condemned and finally closed for good with the opening of the larger and more elegant West Theatre in 1908. Since then, the space has often been remodeled and used as business offices, a hotel, and apartments for retirees. One reminder of the theatre's golden days is the elegant facade with its fine incised sandstone on the second-floor columns; the facade was fully renovated in 1976. Today the structure is on the National Register of Historic Buildings.

Early photograph of the Jaffa Opera House, dated between 1900 and 1910. The Jaffas sold the theatre in 1895, and the name above the entrance was changed early in the century to Trinidad Opera House, as it appears today.

AUTHORS' COLLECTION

OURAY

Wright Opera House

OPENED: DECEMBER 4, 1888

CURRENTLY A MOVIE THEATRE

Ouray, a jewel of a town surrounded by 13,000-foot mountains and nestled in a narrow valley along the Uncompahgre River, was founded in July 1875 by Augustus W. Begole who, with his partner, Jack Eccles, discovered large mineral deposits in the area. The town was named after Chief Ouray of the Uncompahgre Utes; the lovely word "uncompahgre" is of Ute origin and means reddish waters or warm springs, in reference to the numerous hot springs in the region. Shortly after its founding, the town was surveyed by Herbert W. Reed and laid out in the neat rectangular pattern that prevails today. What became known as the Begole Mineral Farm fueled the economy of the new town and drew 864 silver miners and other residents by 1880. Yet, as a visitor wrote that year, "If the miners of Ouray pray at all, it is for the coming of the Iron Horse."[21] It was not till 1887 that the Denver & Rio Grande Railroad was extended thity-six miles from Montrose to Ouray, which ensured the town's future and led to another burst of growth and prosperity.

Local historian Doris H. Gregory describes Ouray in 1888 as "a rough frontier mining town with two newspapers, four churches, innumerable saloons, a well-established and thriving red-light district and a population of over fifteen hundred."[22] Into this community, H. E. (Ed) Wright and his wife, Letitia, wished to introduce greater cultural opportunities as well as a showcase for their talented nine-year-old daughter, Irene. Wright, a Canadian by birth, had moved to Ouray in 1875 with his brother, George, and struck it rich at the aptly named Wheel of Fortune Mine, which they sold in 1877 for $160,000. That money helped to finance construction of the Wright Building in 1881, an impressive structure located on the corner of Third Street and Fifth Avenue; it was used primarily as a clothing store. Seven years later, construction began on "Wrights Hall" (the name is still visible below the pediment), which adjoined the south side of the Wright Building, at 340 Third Street. The theatre occupied the second floor, the first floor being used for storerooms, soon leased to the San Juan Hardware Company.

Exterior of the Wright Opera House, Ouray (date unknown). The theatre is on the second floor of the larger building on the left, with access via the stairway.
PHOTO COURTESY DENVER PUBLIC LIBRARY, WESTERN HISTORY COLLECTION, X-12829

Built of stone and brick, a relatively new building material for Ouray in 1888, the opera house occupied a space 47 feet wide and 77 feet deep. With its decorative, pressed-metal facade, five large windows, wrought-iron balcony, and stained-glass window directly above the center window, it was considered one of the handsomest buildings in town. One entered the opera house through a doorway on the north side, then climbed a stairway to the ticket office. Inside, the auditorium could seat 500 on removable seats. The stage was small, approximately 20 feet deep and 48 feet wide, with a proscenium opening only 22 feet across and 12 feet high. (Shortly after the opening, the stage was enlarged slightly and a gallery added to the auditorium.) Especially noteworthy was the drop curtain, painted by an artist associated with one of the Tabor theatres, depicting

H. E. (Ed) Wright (1849-1895), owner and builder of the Wright Opera House.
DENVER PUBLIC LIBRARY, WESTERN HISTORY COLLECTION

Mt. Sneffels as seen from the Dallas Divide, based on a William H. Jackson photograph. The famous local newspaper, the *Solid Muldoon*, called the illustration "as grand a landscape as America affords;"[23] the curtain is now stored in the basement. Also extant is the front curtain, by C. H. Doxsee, which portrays a scene in Venice, framed by painted marble columns and gold-fringed draperies, and the more prosaic advertisements or "business cards" of local merchants.

Despite the many attractive features of the opera house, its opening drew little fanfare. On December 4, 1888, Ouray's Magnolia Band gave a benefit concert and ball to pay for new uniforms. The *Muldoon* entreated, "Every citizen of the county should attend and give the band boys a good send off."[24] No record exists of the first-night attendance and reception, but the opera house, under Ed Wright's management, soon hosted other concerts as well as theatre. In August 1889, the touring Vincent Company presented a series of dramas and comedies, but the audiences were small, which the newspaper found "truly demoralizing:"

> Standard plays were given and acted in a manner to win applause
> from metropolitan critics. But 'twas no use. Leg dramas, circus and
> minstrel shows catches Ourayites[,] as witness the circus for a thou-
> sand dollars. The MULDOON regrets this but there is no account-
> ing for taste.[25]

During the appearance of the Vincent Company, the theatre was saved from disaster by an alert night watchman who, at 3:00 in the morning, found that a burning candle had ignited a property chair and one of the stage borders. He quickly extinguished the blaze, and as the paper reported, "The loss will not amount to $15, but the mysterious burning candle and the time of morning will haunt Ed Wright for many a day. It was a close call for the Opera House."[26]

Too remote to become part of the Silver Circuit, Ouray had to take advantage of whatever theatrical entertainment offered itself, not all of which was high in quality. On March 15, 1889, the *Muldoon* railed against Stetson's *Uncle Tom's Cabin* Company. The performance drew a large audience paying $1.25 for reserved seats, which the paper considered "grand larceny. The show in its entirety was fourth rate. . . . All told, the dogs were the best performers, and they were chained."[27] The local critic was even more agitated two years later at the impending arrival of the McFadden *Uncle Tom's Cabin* Company:

> Ouray has been visited in the past by more fake shows and stood up
> under the affliction better than any other town in the state, and for

*this good nature has been dubbed among the class of hams who over-
run Colorado the "sucker" town of the San Juan. We are "passed
around" from one fakir [sic] to another and have been robbed until
patience has ceased to be a virtue, and there is a howl now to go up
from which there will be no cessation until the evil has been corrected
and the management of the opera house here sits down hard upon
the bum so called theatrical outcasts who make this village a means
of revenue from which to eke out an existence.*[28]

Even so, the theatre continued as the center of Ouray's cultural and
social life. It did not suffer its first serious blow until July 7, 1895, with the
unexpected death of its owner, Ed Wright, from pneumonia contracted
while working with his brother at the nearby Grizzly Bear Mine. His
widow, Letitia, with the help of a $2,000 life insurance payment, took over
as manager and immediately repaired the theatre's exterior and remodeled
its stage and scenery. In support of her management, the *Ouray Herald*
congratulated her at the completion of her first season:

*... one of the finest opera houses in southwestern Colorado. That Mr.
Wright's judgment was good is evidenced by the fulfillment of his hopes*

Stage of the Wright Opera House, October 1891, with the cast from the play
Queen Esther.

PHOTO COURTESY DORIS H. GREGORY

*of having attracted to Ouray many of the best theatrical companies vis-
iting Colorado and by managers having found Ouray audiences so
appreciative as to justify their return from season to season.* [29]

Letitia's management was to be short-lived, for in February 1898 she
lost the theatre to a creditor of her late husband's. Two months later, on
May 2, 1898, it was bought back by Ed's elder brother, George, who thus
kept the Wright Opera House in the family for the next seventeen years.

With the assistance of his business partner, David Frakes, Wright
opened his theatre to more than touring companies, minstrel shows, musical clubs, dances, and high-school graduations: it also hosted noted speak-
ers like Samuel Gompers, founder of the American Federation of Labor,
who described the A.F.L. and recruited members at a speech given on
May 25, 1899; and Eugene V. Debs, head of the Socialist Party, who spoke
there in 1902 and returned four years later. Motion pictures were also
shown, beginning in 1906. Closed by a devastating flood in 1909, the
opera house recovered and continued to be used mainly for dances and
local presentations until George Wright sold it to the local Masons on
May 21, 1915. He died the following year, on December 21, 1916.

Since that time, the opera house has remained a community center and entertainment venue for Ouray under various owners.
Purchased in 1965 by Francis L. and Mary E. Kuboske, the old theatre
was officially reopened in 1977 by country and western singer C. W.
McCall. The Wright was purchased in the 1990s by Alice and Larry
Leeper, who received a State Historical Fund grant to rehabilitate the
building. The facade has been restored and the stage extended in the
hope that live theatre will someday return to the Wright. In the mean-
time, the opera house shows films and hosts a variety of special events.

SALIDA

Salida Opera House

OPENED: JANUARY 1, 1889

CURRENTLY A MOVIE THEATRE

Salida was a town born not from gold or silver mines, but from the railroads. In the spring of 1879, the Denver & Rio Grande Railroad won the "Royal Gorge War" and was granted permission to expand its narrow-gauge line from Pueblo, through the Arkansas River Valley and the Royal Gorge, then on to Leadville, Gunnison, and the Western Slope of Colorado. By May 20, 1880, the line had arrived at South Arkansas (the original name of the town), and the station was open for business. When the post office department objected to the town's name, Governor Alexander C. Hunt suggested Salida, the Spanish word for "outlet." Under its new name the town was officially incorporated on October 4, 1880.

In June 1880, Salida's recorded population was only 353, but as it became a division town for the railroad and a distribution point for mining towns in the region, Salida grew steadily during its first decade to 2,586 residents by 1890. In February 1882 its first opera house was opened by a lumber dealer, Herman Dickmann, and his son, Max, on the second floor of a two-story frame building. It burned down on January 2, 1888. Five months later, the Salida Opera House Association was formed by about thirty businessmen to raise $30,000 for construction of a new opera house, and capital stock for that amount was easily sold. E. W. Corbin, the head of the building committee, selected and purchased a plot of ground 75 feet wide and 150 feet deep, and construction plans were hurriedly approved so work could begin in the summer. The contract was awarded to the firm of Chenowith and Johnson, which had recently built the Glenwood Springs Opera House, and construction began on August 1, 1888.

The local newspaper reported that "critics are on the ground every day telling how they would build the new opera house."[30] Whether or not their advice was taken, what they saw emerge was a fine, sturdy theatre at what is now 125-131 West First Street, with a 75-foot frontage, length of 110 feet, and a brick exterior punctuated with windows and stone cornices. "It will not be pretentious, nor a huge, overgrown sort of a structure," wrote a local newspaper of the building that eventually cost $25,000, "but it will be neat and cosy, and of ample proportions for the needs of our people—for the present at least."[31] The two most striking features from the outside were the grand entrance, a Roman arch 21 feet wide, flanked by stone pillars and fronted by an iron gate; and a large pediment directly over the entrance, 48 feet above the ground.

The interior, too, was more functional than ornate. The downstairs portion of the auditorium, 80 feet long and 50 feet wide, could seat 400 and consisted of a flat parquet with removable chairs (so it could double as a dance floor), a sloping dress circle, and two boxes, one on either side of the stage. Overhead, the balcony, which could accommodate 350 people, curved around the side walls of the auditorium until it joined two boxes directly above those on the main floor. The ceiling was 27 feet high from the center of the auditorium, and a series of windows on either side provided ample light and good ventilation. The drop curtain

Exterior of the Salida Opera House (date unknown).

The only known photograph showing the original exterior of the Salida Opera House (date unknown).

depicted lovers on the street canals of Venice, and new scenery had been painted for the stage, which measured 50 feet across but only 30 feet in depth, with a proscenium opening 25 feet wide and 15 feet high.

For the grand opening of what was called "the second best opera house in the State"[32] (next to the Tabor Grand in Denver), 250 people paid the extravagant amount of $5.00 a ticket to attend a ball on New Year's Evening, 1889. Red, white, and blue flags were draped around the walls and stage, a modern furnace heated the interior, and seventy-five electric bulbs so illuminated the auditorium that "the guests upon coming into the room from the darkness of the street felt as if suddenly transported to fairy-land."[33] With music provided by Professor Simon's Leadville Orchestra, those in attendance danced from 9:00 to midnight, retired to the Monte Cristo Hotel for dinner, then returned to the opera house for more dancing until 3:00 a.m.

This gala event was succeeded by the first theatrical performance on January 16, 1889, with the Park Dramatic Company presenting Robert Buchanan's drama, *Alone in London.* A standing-room-only audience, consisting of men and women in formal dress as well as "the pick and shovel brigade" in the balcony, greeted the rising of the curtain with deafening applause. F. E. Gimlett, who bought the opera house twenty-five years later, enjoyed the play but objected to many of the men dashing out of the theatre between acts for a cigar or a drink at a nearby

Interior of the Salida Opera House, July 4, 1890.

saloon, then stumbling over their female companions as they groped to their seats after the next act had started: "I wondered then and I wonder now, as I look at the average male and a jackass, if there can be any doubt as to the biggest jackass of the two."[34] Whatever the off-stage distractions, the performance was completely satisfying, and the "opening of our Opera House was, to us, as great an event as the opening of the Tabor Grand Opera House was to Denver."[35]

As the first manager of the opera house, E. W. Corbin instituted some policies that remained in effect through its first decade. Prices were set at the popular rates of 30 cents for the parquet, 20 cents for the balcony, and 10 cents for the gallery. Also, he immediately established Salida as a one-night stop on the Silver Circuit. The first year featured such stars as Effie Ellsler in *Judge Not* and Frederick Warde in *Damon and Pythias*, an *Uncle Tom's Cabin* company, the ever-popular minstrel shows, and such spectacles as Lilly Clay's Gaiety Company in *Beauty in Dreamland*, with "Forty of the Handsomest Ladies in the World," perfectly respectable "with the exception, perhaps, that the female performers wore tights."[36] Occasionally a local critic would carp at the audience's supposed lack of discrimination in preferring some productions over others:

It seems almost impossible to induce our people to attend a strictly first-class and highly meritorious theatrical performance. But let "Uncle Tom's Cabin" or a snide circus come along and they would all go if it became necessary to pawn the cook stove for admission money.[37]

Because the Silver Circuit did not convey productions to Salida in the summer, Corbin kept the theatre open by booking repertory companies for week-long engagements. Although these companies did not have the advantages of star actors, beautiful scenery and costumes, and new plays, the members took time to mingle with the townspeople and promote their performances through word of mouth as well as raffles and door prizes, usually with success.

On December 29, 1889, almost a year to the day since the grand opening, Corbin died suddenly of a heart attack at age thirty-five. His place was taken by A. R. Rose, who followed most of Corbin's practices. Musical comedies, spectacles, and minstrel shows continued to be popular. Meanwhile, attractions from the Tabor Grand and the Broadway in Denver were especially appealing to Salida's audiences, with Robert Mantell in *Othello*, Thomas Keene in *Richard III*, and Rose Coghlan in *Peg Woffington* appearing at the opera house via the Silver Circuit in the early 1890s.

Even so, Salida faced certain problems not encountered in the larger cities. For example, visiting companies would sometimes substitute understudies for their stars, or present a condensed version of a play, especially if the theatre was poorly attended—the better to catch the night train out of town. About a performance of *The Clenenceau Case* on January 6, 1892, a reviewer complained that while the play was "deep and feeling" when seen in its entirety,

on this occasion it was so badly slighted that people who had seen it before could hardly recognize it. Some of them [the actors] did not even take the trouble to change their costumes; the performance was hurried through which no doubt was from the discouragement caused by the small house.[38]

Also, although audiences were generally well mannered, the gallery-goers could sometimes be rowdy and disruptive. When Katie Putnam was performing in *Erma, the Elf* on January 20, 1890, "three or four young men disgraced themselves by loud and boisterous talking, cat calls and other unseemly noises. . . . Their performances are disgusting, and should not be tolerated by the management."[39]

When A. R. Rose resigned as manager early in 1895 to become a traveling gun salesman, his place was taken by George W. McGovern, one of the leading businessmen of the town and a former mayor. McGovern liked to use his name as a personal endorsement in opera house publicity, even offering money back guarantees for some performances. He also lowered ticket prices from previous levels, and perhaps for this reason was reluctant to book any show that required a large guarantee. He decided to engage Katie Putnam in *The Old Lime Kiln* because "Salida has not had an entertainment of this class for nearly two months,"[40] but her performance on April 1, 1896, drew only an average audience. The reviewer judged that "considering the merit of the entertainment the patronage should have been better, but a small house is the usual fate meted out to any company appearing in Salida."[41]

Having been burned once too often in this way, McGovern increasingly turned to farces, musical comedies, sensational melodramas, and the ever-popular minstrel shows, and away from the more expensive stars and productions. If he did consent to engage a high-class entertainment, he would sometimes advertise the extent of the guarantee, adding that if an insufficient number of tickets were sold in advance, the show would be canceled. Not all of McGovern's austerity measures were appreciated, least of all his habit of firing the furnaces at the last possible moment. Of a performance in January 1899, a reviewer reported, "As it was the people wore their wraps and overcoats while the actors shivered from cold and almost choked with the smoke from the furnaces."[42]

The Salida Opera House continued to be used as a theatre after the turn of the century, but in 1909 it was remodeled to accommodate motion pictures and renamed the Osos Grand Theatre. Live performances alternated with movies at first, and continued to be presented as late as April 1936, when the theatre was fully converted to a movie house, called the Salida Theatre. One memoirist who recalled the theatre's glory days wrote in 1948, "Today the massive brick work and trustled [trussed?] roof of the SALIDA OPERA HOUSE still stands and marks the initiative and confidence of a people afflicted with a 100% supply of civic pride and faith enough in a community to take a chance."[43] During the 1960s the building was remodeled inside and out and renamed the Unique Theatre, under which name it continues to operate as a movie house today.

GRAND JUNCTION

Park Opera House

OPENED: JUNE 23, 1892

CLOSED: c. 1912

DEMOLISHED: 1934

Since its founding on October 10, 1881, Grand Junction has been the major commercial and cultural center of Colorado's Western Slope. A group of land speculators, led by ex-Kansas governor George A. Crawford, established the town site at the confluence of the Grand (now the Colorado) and Gunnison Rivers. With such an abundant water supply for irrigation, the region developed into one of the state's leading agricultural areas, especially notable for its vegetables, fruits, and grains. But it was the railroad that first put the town on the map. The Denver & Rio Grande Railroad (the Black Canyon line) arrived from Salida, Gunnison, and Montrose on November 25, 1882, and other lines followed. As a result, the town grew from about 200 log cabins and a population of 250 in 1882 to a major community of 2,030 citizens in 1890.

Practically from its inception, Grand Junction had its places of amusement, including the Mesa Opera Rink, built in 1885, whose very name reveals the multiple purposes these halls served. But as in other Colorado towns, a corporation was formed in 1891 for the express purpose of financing and erecting an opera house that would serve as both a community center and a symbol of civic pride. Orson Adams, Jr., the secretary and treasurer of the corporation, and its president, C. W. Steele, were the driving forces behind this effort, and by August 1891, the necessary financial support of $25,000 had been obtained, a site chosen (previously occupied by a livery stable), and plans approved. Construction was underway by November 1891.

Unlike most opera houses built in the smaller Colorado towns, Grand Junction's was to be a truly imposing structure, three stories high and built of brick, so it "towers high above all the buildings of the city."[44] Facing Ute Avenue close to the corner of Fourth Street, the theatre was situated across the street from the appropriately named Cottonwood Park (now Whitman Park), from which the opera house derived its name.

The only known photograph of the Park Opera House, Grand Junction (date unknown).
PHOTO COURTESY MUSEUM OF WESTERN COLORADO, 1983.7

While the exterior was large and handsome, it was the ornate interior that most impressed the 600 playgoers who attended opening night on June 23, 1892. Designed by architect J. J. Huddart, the building displayed a beautifully decorated foyer, a two-level auditorium (parquet and dress circle below, balcony and gallery above), first-class opera chairs in all sections except the gallery, and electric lighting. The splendid stage, 65 feet wide and 33 feet deep, behind a proscenium arch 30 feet wide and 20 feet high, featured a lovely curtain showing "The Bay of Naples" and new scenery painted by Sosman and Landis of Chicago, "who have provided the scenery for nearly all the large amusement houses in the west."[45] The reviewer for the *Grand Junction News* expressed the delight and pride that must have been widely felt:

> *To say that our people are proud of our new opera house is but a tame expression. It is magnificent—a surprise, in beauty and arrangement, both to show people and to our own citizens. There is only one house on the Western Slope that has cost more money—the Wheeler opera house in Aspen—and with all due respect to Aspen, it is far inferior to ours in beauty and the perfect thoroughness of equipment.*[46]

The opening night entertainment was provided by Haverly's Mastodon Minstrels from Chicago. Before the show, E. M. Kayne, the leader of the troupe, addressed the audience and expressed "the great surprise and pleasure of his entire company at finding here so perfect a house when they alighted from the cars [earlier that day]. He prophesied that hereafter Grand Junction would be patronized by the best shows on the road."[47] The company then proceeded to give a spirited performance of the blackface comedy, singing and dancing that characterized the minstrel show. One observer was undoubtedly correct that the actors "all seemed inspired by the occasion and did their utmost to please that splendid audience."[48]

The opera house, managed by Edwin A. Haskell, an experienced theatre man, lived up to the prediction that it would attract the leading lights of the day as well as large audiences with its low admission prices of $1.00, 75 cents, and 50 cents. From the beginning, Grand Junction had the tremendous advantage of location, being approximately halfway between Denver and Salt Lake City, so that touring stars and companies could perform rather than miss a night while en route from one city to the other. According to local historian Richard E. Tope, "Advance agents would make contracts at bargain prices to fill in the time going east or west; as a result then for twenty years Grand Junction could almost write its own contract for stage talent."[49] For this reason, the Park immediately became a crucial link in the chain of Silver Circuit theatres managed by Peter McCourt.

However, scheduling could be precarious since many companies, like Haverly's Minstrels, arrived by train on the same day as the performance and were subject to the vagaries of train travel. Estelle Walker Reese recalled going to that "magnificent structure" in her youth, and at 8:00 each winter evening, manager Haskell would stoke the two large furnaces, "whose heat seared those nearby and whose red glow promised warmth to ones not so near the orchestra. At 8:15 the curtain rose (or was raised) promptly if the D. & R. G. had happened to get in on time. If the train was late you only got more for your money as the companies sometimes set the stage for the entertainment of the waiting audience."[50]

In this setting, citizens of Grand Junction enjoyed such performers as Robert Mantell and Helena Modjeska in Shakespeare; Rose Coghlan, Frederick Warde, George M. Cohan in *Forty-Five Minutes from Broadway*; and the Barrymores—in short, most of the great touring stars of that period. In addition, the Park Dramatic Company performed modern dramas and toured nearby towns, and amateur performances were popular during the summer when the theatre was otherwise dark.

For reasons that are not entirely clear, the Park Opera House operated for only about twenty years. Sources imply that it may have ultimately failed because it was never equipped to show motion pictures, which were also responsible for the decline of theatrical touring. The Park was condemned and closed circa 1912, then sold to the school district. Eventually its place as the community's primary entertainment center was taken by the Avalon Theatre, a splendid facility that opened in January 1923, seated almost 1,500, and could accommodate both stage productions and films. The Park was torn down in 1934 as part of a WPA project, and its former site is now a parking lot for the Museum of Western Colorado, which has preserved much of the available information about the opera house.

CHAPTER SEVEN

THE MELODRAMA TRADITION IN COLORADO: A LINK TO THE PAST

Gold Bar Room Theatre, Imperial Hotel, Cripple Creek

MELODRAMA PERFORMANCES: 1948 TO 1997

Butte Opera House, Cripple Creek

THEATRE OPENED: 1897

RESTORED: 2000

MELODRAMA PERFORMANCES: 2000 TO THE PRESENT

Only a few historic Colorado theatres have survived, but Cripple Creek's melodrama tradition forms a living link to a largely forgotten repertory that was vastly popular on the stages of those theatres, both in Colorado and throughout the country. Although of more recent origin than the other theatres discussed in this book, the Gold Bar Room Theatre was just as notable for its place in Colorado history and its contribution to the

Cripple Creek community. As the home of the Imperial Players, one of the longest running melodrama companies in the country, the theatre was recognized by *Time* magazine in 1962 as "the Old Vic of modern melodrama."[1] Its success spawned similar troupes throughout the state and has led to Colorado's continued identification with melodrama, the same entertainment that strongly appealed to the miners and other early settlers who were so hungry for professional theatre.

Following the first major gold strike in January 1891, Cripple Creek was stampeded by so many hopeful prospectors that its population reached 25,000 by 1900. It came to be known as the world's greatest gold camp, as more gold was mined in the surrounding region than anywhere else in the world during the late-nineteenth century. Two disastrous fires in 1896 virtually leveled the town, but during its reconstruction (this time with buildings of brick and stone rather than wood), two opera houses were added: the Butte, rebuilt and inaugurated in October 1897, and the more opulent Grand, which had its debut two months earlier, on August 2, 1897. Becoming a fixture on the Silver Circuit, the Grand Opera House hosted many famous actors and touring companies in a beautifully decorated auditorium seating 1,000 to 1,500 people. One visitor wrote that he "was most agreeably surprised to find a thoroughly first-class theatre that would do credit to a town three times the size."[2] The Grand was destroyed by fire on July 19, 1907.

When on May 25, 1946, newlyweds Dorothy and Wayne Mackin bought the turn-of-the-century Imperial Hotel, located on Third Street a half-block north of Bennett Avenue, they were looking for an interesting and potentially profitable business to operate. One Cripple Creek resident warned them that the previous owners had been forced to close the hotel: "Those people charged $2.00 and $3.00 a night for a room, and who is goin' to pay them prices?"[3] Yet they were intrigued by Cripple Creek's storied boomtown past.

To help make ends meet, the Mackins thought of converting part of the Imperial Hotel into a theatre. Meanwhile, they learned about Cripple Creek's rich theatrical past, as Dorothy Mackin explains:

> *In the process of restoring the property to its former elegance and rebuilding a business, we searched to find a form of entertainment that would have been popular during the heyday of the gold rush. We found articles and advertisements in turn-of-the-century newspapers published in Cripple Creek which gave us a good idea of the entertainments that had been offered at the local opera house. These were almost equally divided among opera, Shakespearean plays and*

melodramas. In addition, the travelling companies presenting these plays almost always featured variety entertainment as well, with singers, dancers, elocutionists and musicians on the bill.[4]

When the Piper Players, a local acting troupe, were looking for a place to perform melodrama, Dorothy invited them to the Imperial in October 1947, where they staged a production in a corner of the dining room. This venture prompted the Mackins to convert the basement of the hotel, previously used for apartments and storage, into a cabaret theatre. With the help of the Piper Players, they refurbished the area in time for opening night of July 3, 1948, when the Gold Bar Room Theatre welcomed audiences for the first time with *Only An Orphan Girl*, also advertised as *Curse You, Villain; or, I'll Be Glad When You're Dead, You Rascal You.*

Although it had only 90 available seats, the new theatre was immediately successful, attracting 4,800 people in its initial eight-week season, and 6,000 the following year. In 1950, the director of the Colorado Springs Civic Theatre, Orvis Grout, began directing the Imperial Players, as the company was now called. That year, attendance rose to 8,000 (often with standing-room-only audiences) over a nine-week summer season.

But it was the work behind the scenes by Dorothy and Wayne Mackin that began to build the reputation of the Gold Bar Room as the premier melodrama theatre in the country. At

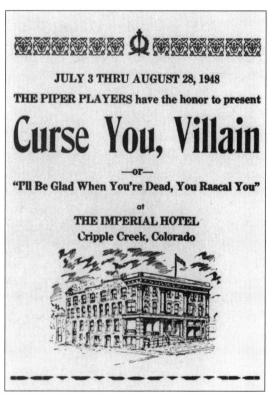

JULY 3 THRU AUGUST 28, 1948

THE PIPER PLAYERS have the honor to present

Curse You, Villain

—or—

"I'll Be Glad When You're Dead, You Rascal You"

at

THE IMPERIAL HOTEL
Cripple Creek, Colorado

Program for *Curse You, Villain*, the opening-season production at the Imperial Hotel in July-August 1948.
PHOTO COURTESY DENVER PUBLIC LIBRARY, WESTERN HISTORY COLLECTION, MSS COLLECTION, F-47934

Scene from *Curse You, Villain*, 1948, starring the Imperial Players.
COURTESY, PIKES PEAK LIBRARY DISTRICT

first they had used modern scripts, called "mellerdrammers," written in the hiss-the-villain style. "Once we began to delve into the field of true melodrama, however," Dorothy wrote, "melodrama as it had been done in the better theatres of the country around the turn of the century, a much more exciting field opened up."[5] Among the wealth of popular melodramas written in the nineteenth century, they found some that were eminently adaptable to a modern audience, including favorites such as *Under Two Flags* (performed in 1961, 1971, and 1984), *The Two Orphans* (1957, 1968, and 1981), *Hazel Kirke* (1954, 1967, and 1983), and *After Dark* (1956, 1972, and 1989). In fact, beginning in 1953 when Bartley Campbell's *My Partner* was presented, the Imperial Players staged only plays written during the period 1840 to 1901, with revivals separated by at least ten years. Scripts, though, were often difficult to find. In 1976, Dorothy Mackin told an interviewer, "You trace down scripts in odd ways. Sometimes you find the name of a melodrama by reading the biography of an old actor or actress and once you have a name you contact sources, collectors, collections in libraries—that sort of thing. There is no easy way."[6] She also thought that "just reading the plays isn't enough—you have to hear how they sound. So I walk up and down and play all the parts out loud for myself."[7]

While undertaking extensive research to locate old play scripts, many of them long out of print, the Mackins also decided to do them "straight," without the burlesque and exaggeration often associated with melodrama. They wanted audiences to appreciate the plays, not simply to cheer, boo, and hiss the villain. For this reason, actors who deliberately changed a line or engaged the audience in any sort of by-play were fined $5.00.[8] Richard Rossomme, a long-time actor and director in the company, stated, "Once you start giving in to the audience you lose sight of the piece. You can't burlesque it because you *believe* it."[9] With some updating, the theatrical values of the plays could appeal just as strongly as they did a hundred years earlier, and the humor, if not done too broadly, could be effective. Dorothy Mackin explained the criteria for choosing a suitable script:

> *The plot and language of the play must be understandable to a wide range of audiences of different levels of education and interest, to children as well as to more mature and elderly patrons. It must be exciting and entertaining enough to hold an audience and keep them enjoying the experience for approximately two-and-one-half hours.*[10]

Wayne Mackin also emphasized that the play should be balanced, with an equal number of roles for men and women.[11] Finally, according to Dorothy Mackin, "They say a good man is hard to find, but it's much tougher to find a really dirty rat. Yet, you can't have a melodrama without a strong villain."[12]

Some alterations in the scripts were inevitable. Dorothy Mackin, who did all the editing, deleted or rewrote crowd scenes that were impractical on the small Imperial stage, clarified archaic language, and revised scenes to make them more comprehensible or producible, thus condensing scripts that originally ran three hours so they could be performed in half that time. But rather than obscure the qualities of melodrama, such changes enhanced it and illustrated the Mackins' central belief that "melodrama is good entertainment, fun for audiences who take its messages seriously as well as for those who ridicule the virtues and vices it portrays."[13] When *My Partner* was first produced in June 1953, a reviewer in the *Cripple Creek Gold Rush* immediately sensed that the Mackins and Orvis Grout had "added something important to American drama:"

> *It is as if the director were standing back and saying "we of the modern generation can laugh at the plays of earlier days much as the*

modern motorist laughs at the horse and buggy days. They were slightly ridiculous, as you can see, but pretty tender and touching, too." And the majority of the audience responded in just that vein.[14]

Ten years later, in a revival of the same play, a reviewer noted, "In contrast to other melodramas in the area,…the actors put as much stress on interpretation of the lines as they do on characterization. There is a definite absence of slapstick exaggeration on the good and bad characters and the overall effect is that of a good drama as well as something at which the audience can have fun hissing and cheering."[15]

The Gold Bar Room Theatre had found its métier, and the seasons were soon extended to a full twelve weeks through the summer, with 150 performances. But success brought its own set of problems, as long lines at the hotel dining room caused subsequent delays in the start of the evening's program. During the winter of 1957-58, the dining room was expanded, while the theatre was continually being remodeled, with the stage being moved back and raised, seats added, and sightlines improved.

Among the actors who performed at their theatre, the Mackins promoted a family atmosphere. Usually they attended university tryouts or regional theatre conferences, where hundreds of actors looking

The production team for the Imperial Players: (L to R) Orvis Grout, Dorothy Mackin, and Wayne Mackin.

Scene from *My Partner*, 1953.

for summer work auditioned for the Mackins and other theatrical producers. Above all, the Mackins looked for "three-dimensional" actors, people who could act, sing, and dance in one of the ten or eleven roles to be cast. In return, they offered their actors better pay than most summer theatres did, as well as room and board. Upon arrival in Cripple Creek, the actors lived in dormitories with the other hotel employees, about seventy-five people in all. Everyone liked the arrangement, although Wayne Mackin recalls, "Sometimes there was too much partying. Our house was too close to the dorms, and we'd wonder, 'Are those people ever going to go to bed?'"[16] Many of the actors who appeared at Cripple Creek later performed successfully on Broadway and elsewhere, and a good number returned to the Imperial Players year after year. Those that acted there five years or more were honored with their own name plaque on a chair in the hotel's Red Rooster Saloon.

With the play and cast selected, the next task was to start rehearsals. The Mackins typically hired a director like Orvis Grout or Robert W. Burroughs, each of whom directed productions at the Imperial for at least twelve seasons, to "get the play on the boards." Dorothy Mackin would then take over supervising the production through the end of the summer. Burroughs, who was head of the Drama Department at the University of Arizona, helped to foster a close association between the

Imperial Players and the university. One of his graduate students, Tom Benson, was set designer for nine seasons, and another student, Richard Hanson, directed the singing and dancing for thirteen seasons. The costumes were designed for twenty-two years by William Damron, Jr., another Arizona product. Each season lasted twelve or thirteen weeks, with twelve performances a week: a matinee and evening show on Tuesday through Saturday, and two matinees on Sunday. Monday was a day off for everyone, and Wednesday mornings were reserved for a rehearsal to work on fine points.

In later years, a typical show began with a sellout crowd of 285 gathering at tables, often with a drink from the bar, to listen to Danny Griffith, musical director and the "King of Melodrama Pianists," play honky-tonk piano. Griffith, who was almost as much a fixture at the Imperial as the Mackins, performed every season for twenty-two years, succeeding such notable pianists as Max Morath and Bob Goodnow. While playing period music that he researched, arranged, and sometimes composed, he helped to establish a rapport between the audience and cast before the curtain rose. This task was much easier at Cripple Creek than at other theatres where he performed because, as he stated, "Our audiences here have come a long way to have fun and they meet you more than halfway. Every performance is fun."[17]

With the audience prepared, the play began. Because the interaction of actors and audience is so integral to melodrama, the Mackins were always striving for the right chemistry, so that playgoers were fully engaged in the performance but not too rowdy. Because of the nature of a cabaret theatre, with drinks available at intermissions, "we kick out lots and lots and lots of people," Dorothy Mackin said.[18] After seeing a production of *The Two Orphans* in 1981, a reviewer wrote:

> *The performance we attended was an unfortunate combination of good acting, good script and an audience primed for "mellerdrammer." Perhaps there is no way to prepare an audience for classic melodrama, but it would have been nice if they had given the play more of a chance before disrupting with boos, hisses, cheers and "suggestions," which are the highlight of the script at "mellerdrammers" but seriously detracted from the fine production on stage at the Imperial.*[19]

But over the course of a season when 40,000 people attended the theatre, such audiences were a minority, and in general they were enthusiastic and often touched by the performances. To sustain a consistent mood throughout the evening, a short vaudeville piece was presented between acts. Finally, after the close of the play, all the actors participated in the olio, a continuous series of vaudeville skits, dances, and songs, with accompaniment by the ever-present Danny Griffith.

In addition to their longevity and high performance standards, the Mackins were justifiably proud of never canceling a performance. As Wayne Mackin explained, "We feel we can't cancel a show when people drive from far away to see it,"[20] and they sometimes went to extraordinary lengths to ensure the show would, indeed, go on. One actor who was so ill he was admitted to the hospital wanted to perform anyway, so Dorothy Mackin shuttled him back and forth from hospital to theatre for three days. When another actor's car broke down in a remote part of the state, the Mackins chartered a plane to fly him in for the next performance.[21] At times, playgoers were called upon to be as resolute as the company. On opening night in 1974, sixteen inches of snow fell, yet 170 of the 270 ticket holders braved the steep and winding Cripple Creek highway to attend the show.

In 1992, after forty-five consecutive seasons at the Imperial, the Mackins sold their hotel and retired. For the next three years, the Imperial tradition was carried on by Richard and Cynthia Rossomme. They produced both traditional melodramas and modern revues and, with the advent of legalized gambling in Cripple Creek, attempted a year-round theatrical season. The fiftieth anniversary of the Imperial Players was marked in 1997 by the return of melodrama—appropriately, one written by Dorothy Mackin, entitled *Four-Legged Fortune*. Beginning in the summer of 2000, son Stephen Mackin and his wife, Bonnie, have revived the classic melodrama tradition in the restored Butte Opera House, fittingly beginning with a production of *My Partner*.

The Butte had withstood a variety of conversions and remodels since its opening in about 1896. At one time and another it housed a dancing academy, skating rink, a garage, and the Cripple Creek fire department. Owned by the City of Cripple Creek, concerted effort to restore the building as a theatre began in 1999. The Butte Opera House Foundation oversees its operation today, leasing the space to the Cripple Creek Players, who continue to offer authentic melodrama there. The company, appropriately enough, is managed by Stacy Mackin, granddaughter of Wayne and Dorothy Mackin.

Meanwhile, the influence of the Imperial Players has been widely felt throughout the region. In 1967, Dorothy Mackin knew of fourteen melodrama troupes playing in Colorado alone, all of them inspired by the Imperial Players. Of particular importance is the Diamond Circle Theatre in Durango, which has been presenting melodrama for over forty years in and near the historic Strater Hotel. Coloradans are indeed fortunate to see these favorite plays of the past performed today, with the same gusto and emotion that made melodrama so entertaining to its frontier audiences.

APPENDIX A

COLORADO'S HISTORIC THEATRES: A CHRONOLOGY

Theatre/City	Opening Date	Cost	Original Capacity	Shared Space With	How Financed	Architect	Stage Dimensions	Current Status
McClellan Opera House, Georgetown	2 July 1869	unknown	200	furniture store	Erskine McClellan	Erskine McClellan	30 wide 50 deep	Burned in 1892
Central City Opera House	4 Mar. 1878	$23,000	750		private capital and public subscription	Robert S. Roeschlaub	40 wide 50 deep	Restored; in use
Tabor Opera House, Leadville	20 Nov. 1879	$30–40,000	800+	saloon druggist, clothing store	Horace Tabor	L.E. and J.T. Roberts	58 wide 35 deep	Still standing; museum
Colorado Springs Opera House	18 Apr. 1881	$80,000	800		I. Howbert, B. F. Crowell, J. F. Humphrey	A.C. Willard & Co	54 wide 30 deep	Bars, nightclubs
Tabor Grand Opera House, Denver	5 Sept. 1881	$850,000	1,500	opera house block	Horace Tabor	W.J. Edbrooke, F. P. Burnham	72 wide 45 deep	Torn down, 1964
Jaffa Opera House, Trinidad	23 Oct. 1882	unknown	710	retail store	Sol, Henry, and Samuel Jaffa	unknown	30 wide 24 deep	Apartments
Wright Opera House, Ouray	4 Dec. 1888	unknown	500	retail space	H. E. Wright	unknown	48 wide 20 deep	In use for special events, movies

	Date	Cost	Capacity	Other use	Financed by	Architect	Dimensions	Status
Salida Opera House	1 Jan. 1889	$25,000	750	Masonic Hall	public subscription	Chenowith and Johnson	50 wide 30 deep	In use as a movie theatre
Wheeler Opera House, Aspen	23 Apr. 1889	$125,000	800	bank, offices clothing store	Jerome Wheeler	W.J. Edbrooke	50 wide 26 deep	Restored; in use
Elitch's Gardens Theatre, Denver	1 May 1890	unknown	600	Elitch's Gardens	John and Mary Elitch	John Elitch	30 wide 20 deep	Undergoing rehabilitation as a theatre
Broadway Theatre, Denver	18 Aug. 1890	$250,000	1,624	Hotel Metropole	M. B. Leavitt, William H. Bush	Col. J. W. Wood	72 wide 40 deep	Torn down, 1955
Pueblo Grand Opera House	9 Oct. 1890	$500,000	1,100	barber shop bank	public subscription	Adler and Sullivan	90 wide 75 deep	Burned, 1922
Park Opera House, Grand Junction	23 June 1892	$25,000	740		public subscription	J.J. Huddart	unknown	Torn down, 1934
Burns Theatre, Colorado Springs	8 May 1912	$350,000	1,400	business offices	James F. Burns	Douglas and Hetherington	65 wide 45 deep	Torn down, 1973

FOR FURTHER READING

The following bibliography, a selection of the materials used in our research, represents a good starting point for any prospective student of Colorado theatre history. Some of these documents do not circulate outside their collections, but many of the books and articles listed here are easily available to the general reader, and we found them especially useful in learning about Colorado theatre and its economic background. Since many of the standard bibliographies do not include some or even most of these sources, we hope listing them here will help to remedy this oversight.

GENERAL

All studies of Colorado theatre necessarily begin with Benjamin Poff Draper's monumental and comprehensive "Colorado Theatres, 1859-1969," 5 vols., Ph.D. Diss., Univ. of Denver, 1969. One of the few articles Draper published on the subject is his "Colorado's Dramatic Hey-Day: Grand Events in Historic Theatres," *Rocky Mountain Life*, July 1948, pp. 26-31. Only one book concentrates solely on Colorado theatre: Melvin Schoberlin's *From Candles to Footlights: A Biography of the Pike's Peak Theatre 1859-1876*, Denver: Old West Publishing, 1941. It deals primarily with the state's pioneer theatre, before the opening of most of the opera houses discussed here. Allen John Adams, "Peter McCourt, Jr. and the Silver Theatrical Circuit, 1889-1910," Ph.D. Diss., Univ. of Utah, 1969, is a useful study of the entrepreneur and his circuit that so dominated Colorado's turn-of-the-century theatres. Robert Vote's "The Early Theatre in Colorado," *Denver Post*, March 20, 1977, pp. 38-45, is well researched and illustrated.

Other sources of Colorado history deal somewhat with the state's theatres. Duane A. Smith's *Horace Tabor: His Life and Legend*, Niwot, CO: Univ. Press of Colorado, 1989, is the standard biography of this famous businessman, politician, and theatre builder. *Stampede to Timberline: The Ghost Towns and Mining Camps of Colorado*, privately printed, 1949, by Muriel Sibell Wolle, recounts the stories of some of Colorado's most famous towns after they had settled into a post-boom quiet. Lucius Beebe and Charles Clegg, *Narrow Gauge in the Rockies*, Berkeley, CA: Howell-North, 1958, offers a good introduction to the well-documented subject of railroading in early Colorado. Robert G. Athearn, *Rebel of the Rockies: A History of the Denver and Rio Grande Railroad*, New Haven: Yale Univ. Press, 1962, profiles Palmer's Baby Road.

Some general works on American theatre devote attention to Colorado's playhouses and performers, especially William C. Young, *Documents of American Theater History. Famous American Playhouses*, 2 vols., Chicago: American Library Association, 1973; David Naylor and Joan Dillon, *American Theaters: Performance Halls of the Nineteenth Century*, New York: John Wiley, 1997; John W. Frick and Carlton Ward, eds., *Directory of Historic American Theatres,* New York: Greenwood Press, 1987; and Gene A. Chesley, "Encore for 19th-century American Theaters," *Historic Preservation* 25 (Oct.-Dec. 1973), 20-24. Although not specific to Colorado, the following works provide useful background on American drama and theatre: Daniel Blum, *A Pictorial History of the American Theatre, 1860-1970*, new third ed., New York: Crown, 1971; Gerald Bordman, *American Musical Theatre,* New York: Oxford Univ. Press, 1978; and Cecil Smith and Glenn Litton, *Musical Comedy in America,* New York: Theatre Arts Books, 1981.

CENTRAL CITY

There are several published histories of the Central City Opera House, including Allen Young, *Opera in Central City,* Denver: Spectrographics, 1993; Charles A. Johnson, *Opera in the Rockies: A History of the Central City Opera House Association, 1932-1992,* n.p.: The Association, 1992; and Charlie H. Johnson, Jr., *The Central City Opera House: A 100 Year History,* Colorado Springs: Little London Press, 1980. Two excellent unpublished sources from the 1960s are Faber B. DeChiane, "Colorado Mountain Theatre: A History of Theatrical Festivals at Central City Colorado from 1932 to 1960," 2 vols., M.A. thesis, Univ. of Minnesota, 1963; and Jesse William Gern, "Colorado Mountain Theatre: History of Theatre at Central City, 1859-1885," 2 vols., Ph.D. Diss., Ohio State Univ., 1960. In the 1930s, two informative articles appeared, one by Charles Bayly, Jr., "The Opera House at Central City," *Theatre Arts Monthly* 16 (1932), 205-[214]; and Lynn Perrigo, "The First Two Decades of Central City Theatricals," *Colorado Magazine* 11 (July 1934), 141-152. Peter McFarlane is the subject of a fine biography by William H. Axford, *Gilpin County Gold: Peter McFarlane, 1848-1929, Mining Entrepreneur in Central City, Colorado,* Chicago: Swallow Press, 1976.

DENVER

Although there are relatively few published sources on the history of Denver theatre, several unpublished Ph.D. dissertations, mostly under the influence of William Campton Bell, have documented this subject, including Bell's excellent "A History of the Denver Theater During the Post-Pioneer Period (1881-1901)," Ph.D. Diss., Northwestern Univ., 1941. Dean G. Nichols,

"Pioneer Theatres of Denver, Colorado," Ph.D. Diss., Univ. of Michigan, 1938, covers the earlier period. Earle W. Winters, "History of the Denver Theatre 1901-1911," Ph.D. Diss., Univ. of Denver, 1957, and Hebron Charles Kline, "A History of the Denver Theatre During the Depression Era, 1929-1941," Ph.D. Diss., Univ. of Denver, 1963, discuss the Denver theatre of this century. Alice Cochran's article, "Jack Langrishe and the Theater of the Mining Frontier," *Colorado Magazine* 46 (1969), 324-37, is an account of "the Father of Colorado Theatre" and his Denver career.

A few studies have been devoted to specific Denver theatres. Elmer S. Crowley has published two articles on the Tabor Grand, the better of which is "The Opening of the Tabor Grand Opera House, 1881," *Colorado Magazine*, 18 (1941), 41-48. Both articles were based on his M.A. thesis, "The History of the Tabor Grand Opera House, Denver, Colorado 1881-1891," Univ. of Denver, 1940. The Broadway Theatre has been comparatively neglected by researchers, but the history of Elitch's Gardens Theatre is thoroughly documented in Edwin Lewis Levy, "Elitch's Gardens, Denver, Colorado: A History of the Oldest Summer Theatre in the United States (1890-1941)," Ph.D. Diss., Columbia Univ., 1960. Caroline Lawrence Dier's biography, *The Lady of the Gardens: Mary Elitch Long*, Hollywood: Hollycrofters, 1932; and Corinne Hunt and Jack Gurtler, *The Elitch Gardens Story: Memories of Jack Gurtler,* Boulder: Rocky Mountain Writers Guild, 1982, are accounts of two long-time managers of the theatre. Although not original in their research, two videocassettes, *Rocky Mountain Legacy: Elitch Gardens,* Dir. Trux Simmons, PBS Video, 1995, and *The Theatre in the Gardens,* Dir. Tom Pade, c. 1991, are enjoyable introductions to Elitch's Gardens and its renowned theatre.

Both the *Denver Post* and *Rocky Mountain News* offer abundant information on the day-to-day activities of these and other Denver theatres.

Leadville and Aspen

Although the colorful history of Leadville continues to beguile those interested in Colorado and mining history, its opera house lacks a painstaking chronicle. The Tabor Opera House's current owner, Evelyn E. Livingston Furman, has written an anecdotal book titled *The Tabor Opera House: A Captivating History*, privately printed, c. 1972. Dorothy M. Degitz, "History of the Tabor Opera House at Leadville," *Colorado Magazine* 13 (1936), 81-89, and her earlier unpublished work, "History of the Tabor Grand Opera House, Leadville, Colorado, from 1879 to 1905," M.A. thesis, Western State College of Colorado, 1935, are interesting, if not entirely reliable, sources.

Leadville boasted a number of newspapers in its early days, but many have disappeared and are available only in quotation in secondary sources. The newspapers devoting most space to reviews at the Tabor were the *Daily Chronicle,* the *Leadville Daily Herald,* and the *Herald Democrat.*

Two unpublished theses provide detailed information on the story of Aspen's Wheeler Opera House. Appearing only a year apart, Kittie Blanchard Riker, "Theatrical Activity in Aspen, Colorado from 1881 to 1893," M.A. thesis, Univ. of Colorado, 1964, and "History of the Wheeler Opera House, Aspen, Colorado, 1889-1894," M.A. thesis, Western State College, 1965, by Bertha Louise Shaw, are helpful, generally reliable sources. Reviews from the *Aspen Daily Times* are more complete than the brief descriptions that passed as criticism in many towns of the time. For overviews of the town's history, see Malcolm J. Rohrbaugh, *Aspen: The History of a Silver-Mining Town, 1879-1893,* New York: Oxford Univ. Press, 1986; and Len Shoemaker, *Roaring Fork Valley,* Silverton, CO: Sundance Publications, 1958. Muriel Sibell Wolle, *Stampede to Timberline: The Ghost Towns and Mining Camps of Colorado,* Chicago: Sage Books, 1949, recaptures the flavor of post-war Aspen.

COLORADO SPRINGS AND PUEBLO

The primary source of information on the Colorado Springs Opera House, and early theatre in Colorado Springs is Jack Duane Barnes, "Simeon Nash Nye, Pioneer Colorado Theatre Manager 1882-1914," Ph.D. Diss., Univ. of Denver, 1972. There is no similar authoritative source for the Burns Theatre. Much of the information on the Burns, and supplementary information on the Colorado Springs Opera House, comes from the files of the Colorado Springs newspapers: the *Gazette Telegraph, Sun, Silhouette,* and *Free Press.* Although it says little about the city's theatres, Marshall Sprague's well-known *Newport in the Rockies,* fourth rev. ed., Athens: Swallow Press, 1987, is the indispensable guide to the history of Colorado Springs.

The history and structure of the Pueblo Grand Opera House have been thoroughly documented in Lloyd C. Engelbrecht's article, "Adler & Sullivan's Pueblo Opera House: City Status for a New Town in the Rockies," *Art Bulletin 67* (June 1985), 277-95. This article is especially rich in photographs and illustrations of the opera house. Other modern studies include David Naylor, "Pueblo's Grand Opera House: Adler & Sullivan's Lost Western Legacy," *Marquee 25* (1993), 1-8; and Madge Gaylord, "Theaters Operated in Pueblo, Colorado during the Nineteenth Century," unpublished paper, c. 1965. The *Pueblo Chieftain* provided much information on the opening of the opera house as well as frequent reviews of its performances.

REPRESENTATIVE THEATRES OF COLORADO

Not surprisingly, the theatres outside the major Colorado cities have been little studied. Roger Charles Klaiber, "An Historical Study of Theatre in Georgetown, Colorado, 1867-1892," M.A. thesis, Univ. of Colorado, 1964; and E. Martin Hatcher, "A History of the Theatre in Gunnison, Colorado, and Salida, Colorado, 1880-1901," Ph.D. Diss., Univ. of Denver, 1969, are authoritative starting points for those towns. F. E. Gimlett's *Over Trails of Yesterday,* Book 7, privately published, 1948, adds details about the Salida Opera House from one of its previous owners. For Ouray, Doris H. Gregory's *The Wright Opera House,* Long Beach, CA: Cascade Publications, 1983, is a carefully researched work written by Ouray's town historian. Trinidad and Grand Junction have not received similar attention from researchers, but local newspapers have provided extensive information on their theatres and performances, particularly the *Trinidad Daily News, Trinidad Weekly News, Grand Junction News,* and *Grand Valley Star.*

THE MELODRAMA TRADITION IN COLORADO

The essential sources of information for the Imperial Theatre are Dorothy Mackin's pamphlet, *The Imperial,* rev. ed., Cripple Creek: Imperial Press, 1987; and her introductions to two play collections, *Famous Victorian Melodramas,* New York: Sterling Publishing, 1982, and *Melodrama Classics: Six Plays and How to Stage Them,* New York: Sterling Publishing, 1982. We also had the great pleasure of interviewing Wayne Mackin in July 1996. (Mr. Mackin passed away on June 13, 2003.) These sources have been supplemented by newspaper reviews and feature articles in the *Cripple Creek Gold Rush, Colorado Springs Gazette Telegraph, Denver Post, Rocky Mountain News, Sun, Free Press, Time,* and *Life.*

In addition, Allen J. Adams, "Mining Theatre History," *Players* 44 (Dec.-Jan. 1969), 62-65, discusses Cripple Creek's colorful theatrical history.

NOTES

CHAPTER ONE

1 Suzanne Schulze, *A Century of the Colorado Census* (Greeley: Univ. of Northern Colorado, 1977), 16.

2 *Admission of Colorado as a State*. 43rd Congress, 1st session, House Report 619 (1873 Census), 4.

3 *Statistics of the Population of the United States at the Tenth Census (June 1, 1880)* (Washington: Government Printing Office, 1883), Table III.—Colorado, 113.

4 Cornelius W. Hauck and Charles Albi, *Colorado Railroads and the Colorado Railroad Museum* (Golden, CO: Colorado Railroad Museum, 1989), 9-12.

5 Alice Cochran, "Jack Langrishe and the Theater of the Mining Frontier," *Colorado Magazine*, 46 (1969), 324-37.

6 Allen John Adams, "Peter McCourt, Jr. and the Silver Theatrical Circuit, 1889-1910," (Ph.D. diss., Univ. of Utah, 1969), 44-64.

7 Ibid., 79-88.

8 Ibid., 88-91.

9 *Rocky Mountain News*, 13 October 1898.

10 Ibid.

11 William Campton Bell, "A History of the Denver Theater During the Post-Pioneer Period (1881-1901)," (Ph.D. diss., Northwestern Univ., 1941), 243-59.

12 Ibid., 225.

13 Daniel Blum, *A Pictorial History of the American Theatre 1860-1970* (New York: Crown, 1971), [4].

14 Charles H. Shattuck, *Shakespeare on the American Stage: From Booth and Barrett to Sothern and Marlowe* (Washington: Folger Books, 1987), 225-43.

15 Marvin Carlson, "Ernesto Rossi in America," in *Theatrical Touring and Founding in North America*, ed. L. W. Conolly (Westport, CT: Greenwood Press, 1982), 5-14.

16 Bell, 245.

17 Cecil Smith and Glenn Litton, *Musical Comedy in America* (New York: Theatre Arts Books, 1981), 35-42.

18 Bell, 255, 305.

19 Robert C. Toll, *Blacking Up: The Minstrel Show in Nineteenth-Century America* (New York: Oxford Univ. Press, 1974), 92-97.

20 Margaret Coel, Jane Barker, and Karen Gilleland, *The Tivoli: Bavaria in the Rockies* (n.p., 1985), 20-23.

21 Leroy C. Van Allen and A. George Mallis, *Guide to Morgan and Peace Dollars* (n.p.: Arco Publishing, 1971), 9-10; Edward Blair, *Leadville: Colorado's Magic City* (Boulder, CO: Pruett, 1980), 173-74.

22 Carl Abbott, Stephen J. Leonard, and David McComb, *Colorado: A History of the Centennial State*, 3rd ed. (Niwot, CO: Univ. Press of Colorado, 1994), 143-4.

23 "Sheridan Opera House," in *13th Annual Telluride Home Tour "Behind Closed Doors"* (n.p.: Colorfest, 1996), [8].

CHAPTER 2

1 Hal Sayre, "Early Central City Theatricals and Other Reminiscences," *Colorado Magazine* 6-7 (Jan. 1929–Nov. 1930), 53.

2 Frank Crissey Young, *Echoes from Arcadia* (Denver: privately printed, 1903), 86.

3 Central City Opera House Association, *Central City Opera: Looking Back Over Sixty Years, 1932-1992* (n.p., The Association, n.d.), 7.

4 Richard R. Brettell, *Historic Denver: The Architect and Architecture, 1858-1893* (Denver: Historic Denver, Inc., 1973), 94.

5 *Rocky Mountain News*, 15 December 1877.

6 Ibid., 27 February 1878.

7 Ibid.

8 Ibid., 5 March 1878.

9 *Daily Register-Call*, 5 March 1878.

10 *Evening Call*, 22 March 1878.

11 *Daily Register-Call*, 23 January 1879.

12 Ibid., 13 June 1879.

13 Ibid.

14 *Daily Register-Call,* 26 July 1879.

15 Ibid., 6 May 1882.

16 Ibid., 24 June 1881.

17 Ibid., 24 November 1883.

18 Peter McFarlane to H. M. Teller, 16 November 1902. American Heritage Center, University of Wyoming.

19 Peter McFarlane, quoted in Faber B. Dechaine, "Colorado Mountain Theatre: A History of Theatrical Festivals at Central City Colorado from 1932 to 1960" (Ph.D. diss., University of Minnesota, 1963).

20 Peter McFarlane to General Film Company, Denver, 1 January 1913. American Heritage Center, University of Wyoming.

21 Peter McFarlane to Mrs. L. A. Kempton, n.d. Lavonne Axford Collection, 8137, Rec. Box 5, Ltr. Box 15. American Heritage Center, University of Wyoming.

22 Quoted in Charlie H. Johnson, Jr., *The Central City Opera House: A 100 Year History* (Colorado Springs: Little London Press, 1980), 39.

23 *Chicago News*, 28 July 1932.

24 Allan Young, *Opera in Central City* (Denver: Spectrographics, 1993), 13.

25 *Dallas Times*, 31 July 1941.

26 *New York Herald Tribune*, 1 August 1948.

27 *New York Journal American*, 14 April 1958.

28 *New York Herald Tribune*, 4 April 1958.

29 *Central City Opera: Looking Back over Sixty Years, 1932-1992*, 13.

30 Minutes of the Central City Opera Association Meeting, *The Association,* 22 November 1940.

CHAPTER 3

1 Quoted in Alice Cochran, "Jack Langrishe and the Theater of the Mining Frontier," *Colorado Magazine* (Fall, 1969), 324.

2 Ibid., 326.

3 Melvin Schoberlin, *From Candles to Footlights: A Biography of the Pike's Peak Theatre 1859-1876* (Denver: Old West Publishing, 1941), 42, 267.

4 *Rocky Mountain News*, 9 October 1860.

5 Smith, 172.

6 Ibid.

7 *Denver Tribune,* 4 September 1881.

8 Ibid.

9 Ibid.

10 Ibid.

11 Ibid.

12 *Denver Tribune*, 4 September 1881.

13 Eugene Crowley, "The Opening of the Tabor Grand Opera House, 1881," *Colorado Magazine* (March 1941), 41-48.

14 *Denver Republican,* 6 September 1881.

15 Ibid.

16 *Rocky Mountain News*, 6 September 1881.

17 Eugene Field, *A Little Book of Tribune Verse* (New York: Grosset & Dunlap, 1901), 196.

18 Benjamin Poff Draper, "Colorado Theatres 1859-1969" (Ph.D. diss., Univ. of Denver, 1969), V: 1976.

19 *Denver Tribune*, 17 April 1883.

20 *Denver Tribune-Republican*, 27 September 1885.

21 *Rocky Mountain News*, 21 April 1887.

22 Elmer S. Crowley, "The History of the Tabor Grand Opera House, Denver, Colorado 1881-1891" (MA thesis, University of Denver, 1940), 191.

23 *Denver Tribune-Republican*, 12 March 1886.

24 *Denver Tribune*, 29 September 1882.

25 *Denver Republican*, 13 April 1890.

26 *Rocky Mountain News*, 22 April 1934.

27 *Denver World*, 14 July 1888.

28 *Denver Post*, 15 March 1903.

29 Ibid., 10 November 1929.

30 M. B. Leavitt, *Fifty Years in Theatrical Management* (New York: Broadway Pub. Co., 1912), 625-626.

31 *Rocky Mountain News*, 19 August 1890.

32 *Denver Republican*, 3 August 1890.

33 Ibid., 19 August 1890.

34 *Rocky Mountain News*, 19 August 1890.

35 *Denver Republican*, 19 August 1890.

36 *Rocky Mountain News*, 19 August 1890.

37 *Denver Post*, 13 May 1897.

38 Ibid., 20 November 1897.

39 Ibid., 9 February 1901.

40 *Denver Times*, 3 March 1901.

41 *Denver Post*, 28 October 1906.

42 Ibid., 28 July 1931.

43 Ibid., 21 January 1932.

44 Ibid., 29 March 1932.

45 *Rocky Mountain News*, 9 April 1934.

46 *Denver Post*, 31 May 1914.

47 Ibid.

48 *Denver Republican*, 2 May 1890.

49 *Rocky Mountain News*, 18 August 1908.

50 *Denver Republican*, 9 December 1901.

51 Ibid., 16 August 1896.

52 *Denver Post*, 20 July 1900.

53 Ibid., 22 July 1912.

54 *Denver Times*, 23 September 1905.

55 Frederic March, interview by Edwin Lewis Levy, 18 March 1952. In Levy, 261.

56 Ibid., 260.

57 Ibid., 261.

58 Arnold. B. Gurtler, "Elitch's Yesterday and Today," *Billboard* (6 December 1930), 95.

59 Corinne Hunt and Jack Gurtler, *The Elitch Gardens Story: Memories of Jack Gurtler* (Boulder, CO: Rocky Mountain Writers Guild, n.d.), 69.

60 Ibid., 72-73.

CHAPTER 4

1 Duane A. Smith, *Horace Tabor: His Life and the Legend* (Niwot, CO: Univ. of Colorado Press, 1989), 74.

2 Quoted in Draper, III:1152.

3 Smith, 106.

4 *Leadville Daily Chronicle*, 20 November 1879.

5 Ibid.

6 *Leadville Weekly Carbonate Chronicle*, 3 January 1881.

7 *Leadville Daily Chronicle*, 18 November 1879.

8 Evelyn E. Livingston Furman, *The Tabor Opera House: A Captivating History* (n.p.: privately printed, c. 1972), 59-60.

9 Edward B. Larsh, *Leadville, U.S.A.* (Boulder, CO: Johnson Books, 1993), 140-1.

10 *Leadville Weekly Herald,* 6 December 1879.

11 *Leadville Daily Chronicle*, 19 December, 1879.

12 Ibid., 14 June 1880, page; 17 June 1880.

13 Furman, 66-67.

14 *Leadville Daily Democrat*, 8 June 1880.

15 Furman, 51.

16 Otis Skinner, *Footlights and Spotlights* (New York: Blue Ribbon, 1923), 118-19.

17 *Leadville Daily Herald*, 14 April 1882.

18 Richard Ellmann, *Oscar Wilde* (New York: Vintage Books, 1988), 205.

19 Ibid., 204.

20 Ibid., 204.

21 *Leadville Daily Herald*, 17 February 1881.

22 Ibid., 20 February 1881.

23 Ibid., 27 September 1882.

24 Ibid., 26 September 1882.

25 Ibid., 26 September 1882.

26 *Leadville Herald Democrat,* 1 January 1887.

27 Ibid., section 4.

28 *Herald Democrat*, 1 January 1891.

29 Dorothy M. Degitz, "History of the Tabor Opera House, Leadville, Colorado, from 1879 to 1905," (M.A. thesis, Western State College of Colorado, 1935), 13-14.

30 Ibid., 15.

31 *Leadville Herald Democrat,* 1 January 1899.

32 Ibid., 12 September 1899.

33 Degitz, 16, 33.

34 Ibid., 17, 19.

35 Malcolm J. Rohrbaugh, *Aspen: the History of a Silver-Mining Town, 1879-1893* (New York: Oxford Univ. Press, 1986), 68-69.

36 Sarah J. Pearce and Roxanne Eflin, *Guide to Historic Aspen and the Roaring Fork Valley* (n.p.: Cordillera Press, 1990), 8, 13.

37 Len Shoemaker, *Roaring Fork Valley,* rev. 3rd ed. (Silverton, CO: Sundance, 1973), 79, 86-87.

38 Draper, I: 253-8.

39 Pearce and Eflin, 29-30.

40 Quoted in Muriel Sibell Wolle, *Stampede to Timberline: The Ghost Towns and Mining Camps of Colorado* (Privately printed, 1949), 239.

41 *Aspen Daily Times,* 23 February 1888.

42 Ibid., 7 December 1888, 6; 4 January 1889.

43 Ibid., 23 April 1889.

44 Ibid.

45 Ibid.

46 Draper, I, 267.

47 Bertha Louise Shaw, "History of the Wheeler Opera House Aspen, Colorado, 1889-1894," MA thesis, Western State College of Colorado, 1965, 44.

48 *Aspen Daily Times,* 21 April 1889.

49 Ibid., 24 April 1889.

50 Ibid., 25 April 1889.

51 Ibid., 20 April 1889.

52 Ibid., 16 July 1889.

53 Ibid., 28 November 1889.

54 Ibid., 12 June 1890.

55 Ibid., 17 June 1890.

56 Ibid., 28 June 1890.

57 Ibid., 5 February 1893.

58 Ibid., 3 February 1893.

59 Ibid., 15 March 1891.

60 Ibid., 6 December 1891.

61 Ibid., 19 February 1891.

62 Ibid., 19 February 1891.

63 Shaw, 72-77.

64 Wheeler Opera House publicity materials, n.d., 1, 3.

CHAPTER 5

1 "Opera in Early Colorado Springs," Program from Colorado Opera Festival, 1986, 38.

2 Quoted in Jack Duane Barnes, "Simeon Nash Nye: Pioneer Colorado Theatre Manager 1882-1914," Ph.D. diss., University of Denver, 1972, 17.

3 Mrs. Gilbert McClurg, "Retrospective Rambles," *Colorado Springs Gazette,* 15 February 1925, sect. 3, 2.

4 Marshall Sprague, *Newport in the Rockies*, 4th rev. ed. (Athens: Swallow Press, 1987), 49.

5 [Colorado Springs] *Daily Gazette*, 14 April 1881.

6 Ibid., 19 April 1881.

7 *Colorado Springs Gazette*, 24 July 1909.

8 "Statement of Receipts at Colorado Springs Opera House, 1881-82," Special Collections, Pikes Peak Library District.

9 [Colorado Springs] *Daily Gazette*, 15 April 1882.

10 Ibid., 28 May 1882.

11 Ibid., 6 April 1884.

12 Ibid., 17 August 1881.

13 *Colorado Springs Gazette*, 5 July 1891.

14 Mary Ann Lee, "Opera: How It Came to Colorado Springs," *Free Press*, 28 October 1962, 11.

15 Quoted in Douglas R. McKay, "Opera in Early Colorado Springs," Colorado Opera Festival Program, 1986, 40.

16 Ibid.

17 Ibid.

18 *Colorado Springs Gazette*, 27 September 1910.

19 Marshall Sprague, *Money Mountain* (Lincoln: University of Nebraska Press, 1979), 60.

20 "Preliminary Report of the Engineering and Scientific Study Consortium on the Burns Theatre and Office Building Complex," Sect. II, [1].

21 [Colorado Springs] *Sun*, 27 October 1972.

22 Ibid., 24 October 1971.

23 "Preliminary Report," Sect. III, [1].

24 Donnie Smith, "The Burns Theatre: Cripple Creek's Contribution to Colorado Springs Culture," [Colorado Springs] *Sun* (Silhouette Magazine), 24 October 1971, 8.

25 *Colorado Springs Gazette Telegraph*, 22 September 1984.

26 Smith, 8.

27 *Colorado Springs Gazette*, 9 May 1912.

28 Ibid., 27 October 1912.

29 Ibid., 9 September 1913.

30 Burns Theatre program, Special Collections, Tutt Library, Colorado College.

31 Burns Theatre program, Special Collections, Pikes Peak Library District.

32 *Colorado Springs Gazette,* 21 March 1922.

33 Ibid., 30 May 1922.

34 Ibid., 14 February 1922.

35 Ibid., 15 February 1923.

36 Ibid., 26 March 1926.

37 Ibid., 5 October 1922.

38 Letter from DeRos Hogue, 28 March 1973, Starsmore Center for Local History, Colorado Springs Pioneers Museum.

39 Letter from DeRos Hogue to Unknown, 28 March 1973, Starsmore Center for Local History, Colorado Springs Pioneers Museum.

40 Quoted in Lloyd C. Engelbrecht, "Adler & Sullivan's Pueblo Opera House: City Status for a New Town in the Rockies," *Art Bulletin*, 67 (1985), 277-95, quotation on 278.

41 *Pueblo Daily Chieftain,* 10 October 1890.

42 Ibid., 13 May 1888.

43 Ibid., 17 May 1888.

44 Frank Hall, *History of the State of Colorado*, 4 vols. (Chicago: Blakely Printing, 1891), III, 484.

45 Quoted in Engelbrecht, 284.

46 *Colorado Springs Gazette*, 10 October 1890.

47 Quoted in Engelbrecht, 281.

48 *Pueblo Chieftain*, 10 October 1890.

49 *Colorado Springs Gazette*, 10 October 1890.

50 *Pueblo Chieftain*, 10 October 1890.

51 *Pueblo Daily Chieftain*, 15 March 1893.

52 *Pueblo Chieftain*, 17 January 1912.

53 *Pueblo Daily Chieftain*, 30 August 1893.

54 Ibid., 30 September 1899.

CHAPTER 6

1 *Colorado Miner*, 3 July 1869.

2 *Georgetown Courier,* 5 September 1891.

3 Ibid., 10 March 1881.

4 *Colorado Miner,* 1 August 1872.

5 Ibid., 8 August 1872.

6 *Georgetown Courier,* 6 March 1879.

7 Ibid., 11 May 1882.

8 Ibid., 6 May 1880.

9 Ibid., 25 December 1884.

10 Ibid., 14 January 1886.

11 Interview with Sol Jaffa, 23 December 1933, taken by A. K. Richeson, 2.

12 *Pueblo Chieftain*, 1 November 1878.

13 *Trinidad Daily News,* 17 June 1882.

14 Ibid.

15 Ibid., 26 October 1882.

16 Interview with Sol Jaffa, 3.

17 *Pueblo Chieftain*, 18 November 1984.

18 *Trinidad Weekly News*, 11 November 1882.

19 *Trinidad Daily News*, 12 January 1883.

20 Ibid., 14 January 1883.

21 Quoted in Draper, IV: 1351-2.

22 Doris H. Gregory, *The Wright Opera House* (Long Beach, CA: Cascade, 1983), 3.

23 *Solid Muldoon,* 14 December 1888.

24 Ibid., 30 November 1888.

25 Ibid., 9 August 1889.

26 Ibid., 2 August 1889.

27 Ibid., 15 March 1889.

28 Ibid., 12 June 1891.

29 Quoted in Gregory, 31.

30 *Salida Mail*, 7 September 1888.

31 Ibid.

32 *Salida News*, 24 December 1888.

33 *Salida Mail*, 4 January 1889.

34 F. E. Gimlett, *Over Trails of Yesterday*, Book 7 (Published by the author, 1948), 29.

35 Ibid., 27.

36 *Salida News*, 1 August 1889.

37 *Salida Daily News*, 12 July 1889.

38 *Salida Mail,* 8 January 1892.

39 *Salida News*, 3 February 1890.

40 *Mountain Mail*, 27 March 1896.

41 Ibid., 3 April 1896.

42 *Salida Mail,* 27 January 1899.

43 Gimlett, 37.

44 *Grand Valley Star*, 25 June 1892.

45 Ibid.

46 *Grand Junction News*, 25 June 1892.

47 Ibid.

48 *Grand Valley Star*, 25 June 1892.

49 Richard E. Tope, *Objective History: Grand Junction, Colorado* (Musuem of Western Colorado, 1982), 54.

50 *Grand Junction Daily Sentinel*, 12 July 1931.

CHAPTER 7

1 *Time*, 10 August 1962, 45.

2 F. W. Carstarphen, *Dramatic Mirror*, 4 September 1897, quoted in Allen J. Adams, "Mining Theatre History," *Players*, 44 (1969), 65.

3 Dorothy Mackin, *The Imperial*, rev. ed. (Cripple Creek: Imperial Press, 1987), 18.

4 "Introduction" to *Famous Victorian Melodramas*, adapted by Dorothy Mackin (New York: Sterling, 1983), 5.

5 Mackin, *The Imperial*, 27.

6 *Rocky Mountain News*, 30 May 1976.

7 *Denver Post*, 11 August 1963.

8 *Time*, 10 August 1962, 45; *Sun*, 19 June 1981, 17.

9 Unidentified newspaper clipping, Special Collections, Pikes Peak Library District.

10 Dorothy Mackin, *Melodrama Classics: Six Plays and How to Stage Them* (New York: Sterling, 1982), 18.

11 Interview with Wayne Mackin, 16-17 July 1996.

12 *Denver Post*, 11 August 1963.

13 Mackin, *Melodrama Classics,* 19.

14 *Cripple Creek Gold Rush*, 26 June 1953.

15 [Colorado Springs] *Free Press*, 18 June 1963.

16 Interview with Wayne Mackin, 16-17 July 1996.

17 *Rocky Mountain News*, 6 June 1980.

18 *Rocky Mountain News*, 30 May 1976.

19 *Sun*, 19 June 1981.

20 Wayne Mackin in discussion with the author, 16-17 July 1996. Mr. Mackin died on 13 June 2003.

21 *Colorado Springs Gazette Telgraph*, 4 June 1977.

INDEX

Abbott, Emma, 22, 57-59, 62, 92, 93

Adams, Maude, 72

Adler and Sullivan (Architectural firm), 133-4, 181

Alamosa, Colorado, 26

Apollo Hall (Denver), 51-52

Aspen, Colorado, 15, 98-110

Aspen Institute, 109

Aspen Music Festival, 109

Atchison, Topeka & Santa Fe Railroad, 13, 16, 89, 132, 149

Avalon Theatre (Grand Junction), 168

Ballad of Baby Doe, The (Latouche and Moore), 47-48

Barrett, Lawrence, 19, 20, 37, 60, 61, 62, 92, 104, 118

Barrymore, Ethel, 71, 130

Baxter, Oliver H. P., 133, 139

Bayer, Herbert, 109

Belvidere Theatre (Central City), 31

Bernhardt, Sarah, 19, 59, 69, 70, 78, 116, 140

Bland, Sharon and Bill, 96

Booth, Edwin, 19, 20, 60-62, 104

Bostonians, 18, 106

Boucicault, Dion, 20-21, 39, 87

boxing matches, 18, 39, 105, 121

Broadway Theatre (Denver), 62, 63, 64-72, 77, 82, 163, 181

Brown Palace Hotel (Denver), 64, 69

Buckingham, Fannie Louise, 35, 91-92

burlesque, 22, 24

Burnham, F.P., 53

Burns, James Ferguson, 122-4, 128, 129, 131

Burns Theatre (Colorado Springs), 122, 123-131, 132, 181

Burroughs, Robert W., 175-6

Bush, William, 14, 17-18, 64-65, 69, 70, 88

Butte Opera House (Cripple Creek), 169, 170, 177

California Theatrical Circuit, 69

Camille (Dumas), 43, 45-46, 61, 115-117, 146

Central City, Colorado, 29-50

Central City Opera House, 29-50, 180

Central City Opera House Association 42, 48-50

Chaney, Lon, 119

Chase, Mary, 47

Chenowith and Johnson (Construction firm), 159, 181

Chief Theatre (Colorado Springs). *See* Burns Theatre

circuses, 18, 146, 156, 163

City Hall, Colorado Springs, 112

Clarendon Hotel (Leadville), 17, 85, 88, 95

Claxton, Kate, 36-37, 88, 107, 118, 147

Cochran, W. B., 105, 106, 107-8

Coghlan, Rose, 18, 163, 167

Cohan, George M., 71, 120, 128, 167

Coliseum Theatre (Colorado Springs), 121

Colorado Central Railroad, 13, 146

Colorado Circuit, 118

Colorado Midland Railroad, 16, 19, 99

Colorado Springs, Colorado, 15, 111-131

Colorado Springs Opera House, 112-22, 123, 128, 132, 180

Colorado State Historical Fund, 97, 158

Conried's English Comic Opera Company, 102-4

Corbin, E.W., 159, 162, 163

Crabtree, Lotta, 69, 93, 120

Cragg, James H., 92

Cripple Creek, Colorado, 7, 15, 169-178

Cripple Creek Players, 177

Crowell, Benjamin, 112

Cushman Opera House (Georgetown), 147

Cutler, Robert J., 104, 105, 106

Daly, Augustin, 18, 87, 105

DeMille, Cecil, 78

Dempsey, Jack, 105

Denver, Colorado, 24, 26, 51–82

Denver Municipal Auditorium, 26

Denver & Rio Grande Railroad, 13, 89, 99, 111-2, 132, 149, 154, 159, 165, 167

Denver, South Park, & Pacific Railroad, 13

Denver Theatre, 52

Diamond Circle Theatre (Durango), 177

Dickens Opera House (Longmont), 25

Douglas and Hetherington (Architectural firm), 124, 181

Duff Opera Company, 138-9

Edbrooke, William J., 52–53, 99–100, 180, 181

electric lighting, 40, 68, 101, 135, 137, 139, 161, 166

Elitch, John, Jr., 73, 74-75, 78, 181

Elitch, Mary, 73, 74-75, 77-80

Elitch's Gardens Theatre, 73-82, 181

Elks Opera House (Leadville). *See* Tabor Opera House

Ellie Caulkins Opera House (Denver), 26

Ellsler, Effie, 93, 105, 108, 162

English Grand Opera Company, 120

Erlanger, Abraham, 63

Evans, Anne, 42, 47, 50

Fairbanks, Douglas, 78

Ferguson, Cyrus, 122

Field, Eugene, 59, 61

fires, 16, 109, 119, 134, 140-1, 147, 148, 156, 170

Fiske, Minnie Maddern, 78, 79, 120

Forrester, Nate C., 35, 36, 37

French, Henry W., 133

Frohman, Charles, 16, 18, 107

Furman, Evelyn, 89, 95-96

Gable, Clark, 81

gas lighting, 33, 53, 68, 76, 86, 99, 113

Georgetown, 144-8

Giffin-Neill Stock Company, 69-70
Gilbert and Sullivan operettas, 21, 88, 138-9
Gilpin County Opera House Association, 31, 33, 39, 40, 42
Gimlett, F. E., 161-2
Gish, Lillian, 43, 45-46, 110
Glenwood Springs, Colorado, 14, 105, 159
Glenwood Springs Opera House, 159
Georgetown, Colorado, 144-148
Goethe Bicentennial Convocation, 109
Gold Bar Room Theatre (Cripple Creek), 169-177
Goodnow, Bob, 176
Goodyear, Charles W., 74, 76
Grand Junction, Colorado, 14, 15, 165-168
Grand Opera House (Cripple Creek), 170
Granger, Maude, 115-117, 118
Grant, Ulysses S., 89
Griffith, Danny, 176, 177
Grout, Orvis, 171, 173, 174, 175
Grove Theatre (Alamosa), 26
Gurtler, Arnold B., 81

Hale, Horace, 39
Hampden, Walter, 72, 130
Haverly's Mastodon Minstrels. *See* Haverly's Minstrels
Haverly's Minstrels, 22-23, 38, 88, 107, 167
Hayman, Alf, 16
Held, Anna, 19, 95
Historic Elitch Gardens Theatre Foundation, 82
Hogue, DeRos, 131
Hollister, Florence, 95
Hopkins, Robert, 56-58
Hotel Metropole (Denver), 64-65
Howbert, Irving, 112
Humphey, Joseph F., 112
Huston, Walter, 46

Imperial Players (Cripple Creek), 170, 171-7

Jack Haverly's Church Choir. *See* Haverly's Minstrels
Jaffa Opera House (Trinidad), 143, 149-153, 180
Jaffa, Henry, 149-150
Jaffa, Samuel, 149-152
Jaffa, Sol, 149, 151
Janauschek, Fannie, 38, 147-8
Jeffries-Johnson prizefight, 121
Jones, Robert Edmond, 42-43, 46, 47, 50
Juch, Emma, 22, 68-9

Keene, Rose, 38, 163
Kelly, Grace, 81
Klaw, Marc, 63
Kuboske, Francis and Mary, 158

Lambardi's Italian Grand Opera Company, 22, 70, 140
Lamphere, J. B., 86
Langrishe, Jack, 13-14, 29-30, 37, 51-52, 60, 87, 88, 115
Latouche, John, 47-48
Leadville Chapter of Elks, 95
Leadville Coalition, 97
Leadville, Colorado, 15, 24, 83-97
Leavitt, M. B., 64, 69
Leeper, Larry and Alice, 158
"leg" shows, 36, 106, 156, 162
Little Pittsburg Mine (Leadville), 83
Longmont, Colorado, 25

Mackin, Dorothy and Wayne, 170-7
Mackin, Stacy, 177
Mackin, Stephen and Bonnie, 177
Maddern, Minnie. *See* Fiske, Minnie Maddern.
Mancos Opera House, 26
Mantell, Robert, 20, 69, 71, 93,105, 120, 139-140, 163, 167

March, Frederick, 80-81
Marlowe, Julia, 69, 71, 75
Massman, John C., 33, 49
Matchless Mine (Leadville), 90
Mazeppa (Milner), 35-36, 91, 92
McAllister, Phosa, 88
McCall, C.W., 158
McClellan Opera House (Georgetown), 143, 144-8, 180
McClellan, Erskine, 145, 147, 148, 180
McCourt, Peter, 14-17, 18, 41, 63, 64, 69, 70, 102, 104, 119, 139, 152, 167
McFarlane, Ida Kruse, 42, 47
McFarlane, Peter, 32, 39-42, 50
McFarlane, Will, 32, 50
McGovern, George W., 164
melodrama, 7, 20-21, 43, 52, 96, 170-178
Metropolitan Opera Company, 21-22, 70, 95
Milton Nobles Company, 19, 30, 105
mining, 13, 24-25, 83, 88-89, 92, 98, 106
minstrelry, 18, 22, 36, 75, 93, 94, 107, 118, 120, 146, 156, 158, 162, 163, 164, 167
Modjeska, Helena, 19, 61, 71, 93, 104, 120, 139, 167
Moore, Douglas, 47-48
Morath, Max, 176
Moriarty, John, 49
Moses, Thomas G., 67
Mulvihill, John M., 79-81
My Partner (Campbell), 172, 173-5, 177

National Theatre Owners Association, 129
New York Grand Opera Company, 121
New York Theatrical Circuit, 16
New York Theatrical Syndicate, 18, 20, 63, 69, 78
Nicholson, William, 129, 130
Nye, Simeon Nash, 116, 117-122, 129, 139

O'Neill, James, 69, 78, 93, 119-120

Octoroon, The (Boucicault), 20-21, 39, 52
Ouray, Colorado, 154-158

Paepcke, Walter, 109
Palmer, William Jackson, 13, 89, 111-2
Pap Wyman's Saloon (Leadville), 84
Park Dramatic Company, 161, 167
Park Opera House (Grand Junction), 143, 165-8, 181
Piper Players (Cripple Creek), 171
Plishka, Paul, 49, 50
Portland Mine (Cripple Creek), 123
Pueblo, Colorado, 12, 14, 15, 24, 132-142
Pueblo Grand Opera House, 132-142, 181

railroads. *See names of individual companies*
Ricketson, Frank, 47, 49
Rignold, George, 112, 118
rink theatres, 12, 99, 101, 132, 147, 165
Robert E. Lee Mine (Leadville), 112
Roberts, J. Thomas and L. E., 85
Robertson, T. W., 35, 89
Roeschlaub, Robert, 31-32, 42, 180
Roosevelt, Theodore, 140
Rosa, Patti, 105, 107, 108
Rossomme, Richard, 173, 177
Royal Gorge War, 13, 89, 159

St. Leger, Frank, 47
Salida, Colorado, 159-164
Salida Opera House, 143, 159-164, 181
Salida Opera House Association, 159
Salvini, Tommaso, 20, 59
Sands, Jake, 88
Schilling, Charles E., 75, 76
Shakespeare, William, 20, 38, 41, 52, 59, 61, 71, 72, 79, 87, 92-93, 112, 120, 139-40

Sheridan Opera House (Telluride), 25-26
Sheridan, William E., 38
Sherman Silver Purchase Act, 24-25, 40, 108
Silver Panic of 1893, 16, 24-5, 62, 69, 76, 108, 139
Silver Theatrical Circuit, 14-17, 18, 25, 38, 41, 69, 76, 92, 93, 102, 104, 107, 119, 120, 139, 143, 152, 156, 162, 163, 167, 170
Sinclair, Walter, 42
Skinner, Otis, 19, 40, 72, 89, 90, 139
Smith, Laura D., 62, 69
Sousa, John Philip, 21-22, 71, 95, 120
Spooner-Wallock Stock Company, 121

Tabor Grand Opera House (Denver), 18, 20, 22, 26, 38, 51-63, 64, 65, 69, 77, 82, 96, 99, 112, 118, 119, 133, 135, 161, 162, 163, 180
Tabor Opera House (Leadville), 52, 64, 84-97, 118, 180
Tabor Opera House Preservation Foundation, 97
Tabor, Augusta, 18, 47, 58, 83, 92
Tabor, Elizabeth (Baby Doe) McCourt Doe, 14, 17, 35, 47, 64, 88, 92
Tabor, Horace A. W., 14, 17-18, 26, 35, 47, 52-53, 57-59, 62, 64, 75, 83-86, 88, 92, 94, 96, 98, 119, 132-133
Taft, William H., 140
Teller, Henry, 31, 40
Telluride, Colorado, 25-26
Thatcher, John Albert and Mahlon, 133
Treadmills, 35, 71, 102
Trinidad, Colorado, 15, 149-153
Trinidad Opera House, 152, 153. *See also* Jaffa Opera House
True, Allen, 42, 49
Turnvereins, 24
Two Orphans, The (adapted from D'Ennery), 36-37, 88, 107, 147, 172, 176

Uncle Tom's Cabin (adapted from Stowe), 21, 52, 93, 105, 118, 156, 162-3
Union Pacific Railroad, 16
Unique Theatre (Salida), 164. *See also* Salida Opera House

vaudeville, 18, 19, 22, 38, 63, 74-75, 94, 95, 107, 121, 129, 139, 176-177

Wallack, Lester, 18, 87
Warde, Frederick, 162, 167
Webb, Wellington, 82
Weill, Ralph A., 102-104
West Denver Turn Halle, 24
West, Mae, 47
Weston, L. B. (Mrs. A. S. Weston), 94-95
Wheel of Fortune Mine (Ouray), 154
Wheeler, Jerome Byron, 98, 99, 101, 102, 105
Wheeler Opera House (Aspen), 99-110, 166, 181
White, Frank, 71, 78, 79
Wilde, Oscar, 90-91, 118
Willard, A. C. and Company, 112, 180
Wood, J. W., 64, 181
Wright Opera House (Ouray), 143, 154-158
Wright, Ed, 154, 155-157
Wright, Frank Lloyd, 133
Wright, George, 154, 158
Wright, Letitia (Mrs. George Wright), 154, 157-158

If you enjoyed *High Drama,* you may like reading these other titles from Western Reflections Publishing Co.:

A Quick History of Ouray

A Quick History of Leadville

A Brief History of Telluride

A Brief History of Silverton

Illustrations of Historic Colorado

Silver & Sawdust: Life in the San Juans

The Story of Colorado Wines

Glenwood Springs: The History of a Rocky Mountain Resort

To find out more about these titles and others, visit our web site at www.westernreflectionspub.com or call for a free catalog at 1-800-993-4490.